SLOW BOAT
FROM
CHINA

ADRIAN SPARHAM

SLOW BOAT
FROM
CHINA

A man, a woman and a dog
cruising from Hong Kong to Vancouver, BC

SHERIDAN HOUSE

First published 2006 by
Sheridan House Inc.
145 Palisade Street
Dobbs Ferry, NY 10522
www.sheridanhouse.com

Library of Congress Cataloging-in-Publication Data

Sparham, Adrian.
    Slow boat from China / Adrian Sparham.
        p. cm.
    ISBN 1-57409-217-0 (alk. paper)
    1. Sparham, Adrian. 2. Voyages and travels. 3. Seafaring life.
4. Moonshiner (Sailboat). I. Title.

G540.S667 2006
910.4'5—dc22   2005027336

Edited by Janine Simon
Designed by Keata Brewer

ISBN 1-57409-217-0

Printed in the United States of America

What we call the beginning is often the end
And to make an end is to make a beginning.
The end is where we start from . . .

T.S. Eliot

Contents

Prologue   1

Part One: Hong Kong to Rotterdam
1. Beginnings   5
2. The Challenge   13
3. MOONSHINER   19
4. The San Fernando Race   24
5. Fluke   33
6. Leaving Hong Kong   39
7. Puerto Galera Landfall   46
8. A Close Call   51
9. Heading South   57
10. The Land below the Wind   71
11. Breakdown   82
12. Singapore   89
13. The Pirate Strait   98
14. Langkawi   106
15. The Bay of Bengal   111

16. The Arabian Sea   118

17. Red Sea Adventures   126

18. North into Egypt   136

19. The Mediterranean   144

20. Danger in the Rivers   152

21. Fame in the Canals   161

Part Two: Rotterdam to Vancouver

22. Paying the Piper   173

23. Getting Ready   180

24. Kidnapped   187

25. Ocean Crossings   194

26. West with the Sun   202

27. The Caribbean   208

28. Fighting Headwinds   216

29. The Journey Home   221

Epilogue   228

SLOW BOAT
FROM
CHINA

"I'm dying," said the old man. I looked at him. He seemed tired rather than ill, his face resigned, its lines deeply etched in the late afternoon sunlight which brightened the small hospital room we shared. Karl was in his 70s and had been admitted the previous week for routine surgery. "I know it's true," he said. "Every day I walk down the corridor and I count the steps before the pain in my chest gets bad. Every day the distance gets shorter, and this morning I could hardly walk at all." My predictable words of encouragement reassured neither of us, and our conversation soon slowed as we each retreated into our own thoughts.

As roommates, we couldn't have been more different. I was almost half a century his junior, and had been in excellent health until an errant virus, now in retreat, interrupted my passion for sailing and my career in the aviation industry. Karl had expected to return home soon after his surgery to enjoy the rest of his retirement in pain-free mobility, thanks to a new hip. Our shared room, where I had arrived that morning, had vastly different connotations for each of us. For me, it offered tangible proof that having survived the intensive care unit I was now on the mend, and I could look forward to resuming my life as if nothing had happened. For him, it was the focal point of a shrinking world with declining options.

That evening the head of the hospital's cardiology unit arrived in the room quietly and unannounced. He sat next to Karl, and the two men talked softly together for a long time.

Finally, the doctor rose and briefly put his arm around the older man's shoulders as he said goodbye. Early the next morning I was awakened by a sound from Karl's bed. Moments later he was dead from a heart attack.

When I was discharged a few days later I was met by my wife Lot and we drove together to a nearby beach. It was one of those magnificent spring days in the Pacific Northwest; the sky over Vancouver was an endless expanse of brilliant blue, with tufts of high wispy cirrus mares' tails floating over the distant snow-clad mountains. In the foreground, sailboats in English Bay played amongst the dazzling whitecaps that dotted the sea in the boisterous northwest wind. It was a beautiful and vibrant world into which I felt reborn and which, before doing anything else, I needed to soak up and absorb as a reaffirmation of life. I had known Karl for less than 24 hours, but despite the difference in our ages, circumstances had briefly given us a common bond. I wondered what choices he would have made if our situation had been reversed, and he could have re-lived the years that separated us. Would he have done anything differently? Did he regret unfulfilled hopes and ambitions? It is so easy to let the routine of tomorrow automatically follow the routine of today—to miss doing what we really want to do with our lives because it's easier, in the short run, to repeat the familiar and avoid the risk involved in chasing our dreams.

Eventually I will return, as we all must, to the room I shared with Karl and the next time I will not be the one to leave. The years in between are a gift. That day, on the beach in Vancouver, Lot and I resolved to leave as few unfulfilled dreams as possible in our lives, and out of that resolve came the experiences and stories that make up this book. It is a book about sailing and adventure. It is about following your dreams and the decisions, trade-offs, and sacrifices that must be made to make them come true. Nothing comes without a price, even dreams, and as for decisions—well, the most important rule is never to regret them.

Part One

Hong Kong
to Rotterdam

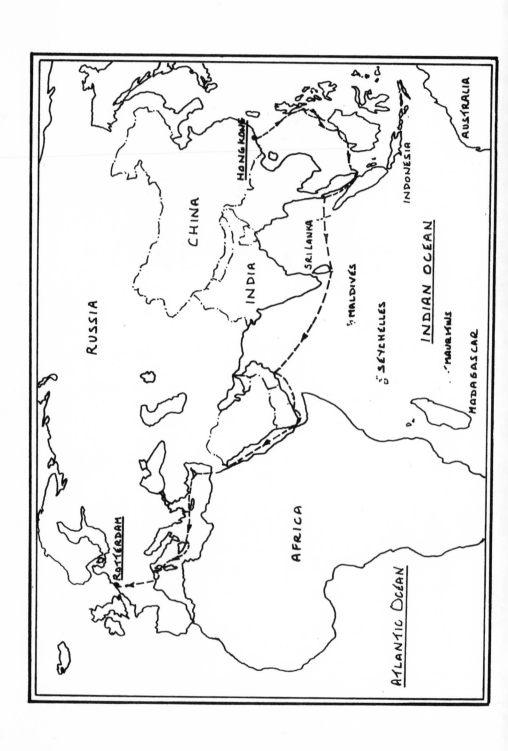

1. Beginnings

As a child growing up in the English coal-mining county of Nottinghamshire, I lived about as far from the sea as it's possible to get, at least in the British Isles. I knew nothing about boats, except that one end was usually more pointed than the other, and none of my friends were any wiser on the subject. No nautical tradition had ever stirred the blood of anyone living in my neighborhood, and if my Aunt Margaret hadn't retired to the coastal resort of Lyme Regis and invited my father and me to spend our summer vacation with her, I would probably have remained a landlubber to this day. But fortune intervened, and our pilgrimage from the industrial Midlands to the Channel coast became an eagerly anticipated annual event. Lyme had managed to avoid the worst excesses that plague coastal holiday resorts the world over; arcades, fast food restaurants, even donkey rides on the beach were thankfully in short supply. In their place the town offered an exquisite mix of scenery, a sixteenth-century harbor, some of the best fossil beds in the world and—most important of all to an eight-year-old visitor— mackerel fishing boats.

Half a dozen mackerel boats competed in the small harbor to take visitors on fishing trips in Lyme Bay. These homespun adventures were a far cry from today's bluewater charters, but to a boy unencumbered by any previous experience of the sea they were magic. The boats were open and gave no protection from the elements. Each was built to a seaworthy design but offered few concessions to comfort; with an overall length of

35 feet they could accommodate up to a dozen customers packed together on hard benches against the hull.

The focus of activity on each boat was a blood-encrusted fetid bucket that dominated the bilge like a galvanized religious icon. Before departure it was used to store ancient hand-lines, complete with rusting hooks and lead sinkers, together with a cork tray holding thin strips of skin cut from fish caught on earlier trips. These shining slivers were used to bait the hooks, but in sufficient numbers they bore witness to each boat's success, and experienced customers took to walking up and down the quay sizing up each boat's supply with a knowing eye. At sea, as soon as a mackerel was caught it was unceremoniously shaken off the hook and into the waiting bucket, where it flailed and gasped—its brilliant mottled colors quickly fading into tarnished silver.

The skippers, their faces burnt brown in the summer sun and fingers gnarled by constant exposure to the brine, wore a uniform of old sea-boots and a soiled roll-neck jersey. They smelled of the sea, and close inspection revealed their clothes, like their boats, to be sheathed in a thin layer of dried sea salt and old fish scales, as if they had surfaced, long ago, from the depths of the ocean. But among the boats competing for my business (at two shillings and sixpence an hour) my favorite, for reasons I can no longer remember, had a skipper with the suspiciously sounding name—even to an eight-year-old—of Captain Crab.

But it wasn't the fishermen, their boats or even the fishing that captured my imagination. It was the excitement of life itself: the sounds, sights, smells and sensations of being a part of the beautiful and restless energy that is the sea. Etched in my mind is the memory of one special day when all the things that it meant to me came magically together. Gulls cried out as they wheeled overhead in a cloudless sky, and sunlight glinted off the whitecaps that broke from the wave crests in a sea of blue and green that seemed to go on forever. In the distance, where the sea met the sky, the cliffs of Golden Cap stood tall against the horizon as the boat rose and fell to the rhythm of the ocean.

Unexpectedly, and for no specific reason, I suddenly felt totally and blissfully happy. Perhaps it is easier for a child, but at that moment I existed totally in the present, with no thoughts of the past or future. Nothing existed beyond the boat, the sea and the sky. I was free—and I was content.

A New Canadian

"Do you have any idea where I could stay in Montreal?" I asked the passenger next to me. Our flight from Manchester was halfway across the Atlantic and I planned to stay in the city that was hosting Expo67 for a couple of days before catching the train to Vancouver. "You could try the Château Champlain," he replied, "it's in a great location and it's a pretty good place." I thanked him, convinced that my accommodation problem was solved. I was a 21-year-old immigrant from Britain—heading to Canada with a one-way ticket and without a job.

The lady sitting behind the welcoming desk for new immigrants at Montreal's Dorval airport was large and friendly. "Do you have anywhere to stay tonight?" she inquired after I told her my plans. "I've been told the Château Champlain's pretty good," I replied, proud of my new international sophistication. "How much money do you have?" she asked with a sudden frown. I told her. "And how are you going to buy food tomorrow?" she inquired under arched eyebrows. She made a reservation for me at a suburban bed and breakfast, and I left the airport, cardboard suitcase in hand and suitably chastened, to explore a new continent.

The thing I remember most about the train trip across the country, other than the fact that the price of beer mysteriously changed every time we crossed a provincial boundary, was a beautiful girl who was heading west after working for the summer swimming in a tank full of dolphins for the entertainment of visitors to Expo. How I envied those aquatic mammals! Sadly, she made it clear that they had achieved a level of watery intimacy with her that I was never going to approach, and dreams of romance on Canada's version of the Orient Express quickly faded. We had a final coffee together at the station in Vancouver before parting to go our separate ways. I paid the bill and checked the money left in my wallet—my total assets. I had exactly $104, no job, no return ticket, the nearest person I knew was 6,000 miles away and I had no idea where I was going to spend the night. To be young is a marvelous thing.

I spent the winter shoveling snow and doing odd jobs at the new ski resort of Whistler Mountain, near Vancouver. The following summer I headed north to the Yukon, where I had obtained work with a mining exploration company. I immediately fell in love with the rugged beauty of western Canada, and spent a total of four more years in mining exploration before eventually returning to Vancouver to attend university. I emerged with a degree in economics and a job in the marketing department of CP Air (later Canadian Airlines). With family and friends living in Europe I thought that the international travel benefits that went with the airline job would be a great way to offset the only disadvantage I saw in living on the west coast of Canada—its relative isolation. And it was also a way of satisfying my passion for travel.

The Dream

"I'm taking my boat out on Saturday afternoon," said an acquaintance. "Would you like to come along?" I was certainly interested. "What kind of a boat is it?" I asked, not knowing if we were talking about a 40-foot powerboat or a canoe. "It's a sailboat," he replied, "a Thunderbird." I had never been on a sailboat in my life and didn't have the slightest idea what a Thunderbird was. Although I had been living on Canada's Pacific coast for over five years the only boat trip I had taken during that time was on a British Columbia ferry. But the idea of a few hours on the water sounded great. "You're on," I replied. It was to be a fateful decision.

His boat was old and in urgent need of repairs, and the day raw and cold with a fickle wind that at times was barely strong enough to breathe life into the sails. But despite the conditions, the experience must have rekindled childhood memories of Lyme Bay; that day marked the beginning of my lifelong love affair with sailing. A week later I enrolled in a beginners' course at a local sailing school, and within a couple of months I was the proud owner of a new 27-foot Catalina sloop that I named CALLIOPE and which became an important part of my life for the next twelve years.

British Columbia has one of the finest cruising areas in the world. Its indented fjord coastline extends over 500 miles from the United States border in the south to the Alaska panhandle in the north and is home to an incredible variety of wildlife, both on land and at sea. Much of the area is sheltered from the open ocean by a series of offshore islands, and for the skipper of any reasonably seaworthy boat the region is a paradise waiting to be discovered. Perhaps it's not surprising that many yachtsmen never feel the need to explore further afield. During the years I owned CALLIOPE I was able to visit only a small portion of it, despite getting out on the water at every opportunity. But cruising to out of the way destinations soon became my passion.

Lot

I ordered a beer and peered across the smoke-filled room, wondering how it was possible to cram so many customers into such a small space and, more importantly, how I was going to get away from the bar without depositing my drink over my neighbors. It was eight o'clock and Café Hathor was already crammed, shoulder to shoulder, with a noisy mix of office workers, professionals, civil servants, artists, and musicians for whom the bar was a regular Friday night hangout in Holland's seat of government, The Hague. The old brick building could remember quieter times; for centuries it had been a tack room—

part of the Dutch royal stables—but the sound of hooves and the smell of horses was long gone.

An hour earlier I had been sitting in my room in another of The Hague's romantic monuments to a bygone age—the famous Hotel des Indes, where Mata Hari had walked the corridors and the ballerina Anna Pavlova had died. My work for the airline often brought me to Holland and des Indes had become a home away from home. I put away my notes from the day's meetings and decided it was time for some R & R. Outside it was cold and blustery, and the cobbled streets, wet and glistening under the streetlights, were almost deserted. The office buildings were empty—their occupants already disgorged into commuter trains or the warm protection of cafés and bars as a prelude to the weekend. I followed the sound of merriment coming from an open doorway, and somehow managed to push my way through the crowd to the bar.

To be a Canadian is to have a friend in Holland—a country that still credits our countrymen for their role in liberating them from the tyranny of Nazi occupation. I found myself talking to a tall blonde girl, with a strikingly short crew-cut hairstyle, who spoke superb English and seemed to know everyone in the place. The beer and conversation flowed freely and I soon felt at home as she introduced me to her friends. Like many good Dutch cafés, Hathor wasn't just a bar but the second home for a regular clientele who viewed one another as members of the same extended family. It was an egalitarian cross-section of Dutch society and the only qualification for membership was the mutual enjoyment of one another's company. The Dutch have never been slow in developing relationships. "Can I take you to diner tomorrow night?" she asked. "What's your name?" I replied. "Lot," she said. "Well, actually it's Charlotte, but everyone calls me Lot."

Her tiny one-room apartment, reached by climbing four flights of narrow stairs, was higher than the surrounding buildings and looked out over the rooftops and chimney pots of the old city like a medieval watchtower. Beyond the small cracked windows, which admitted snow during winter gales, lay a world strangely separate from the city whose sounds rose muted from the streets below. Here, our only neighbors were pigeons and seagulls, and the women who hung out their washing and played with their children on nearby balconies. In the distance, beyond the windswept rooftops, lay the fishing port of Scheveningen, and beyond that the North Sea. An ancient gas fire hissed and spluttered—its cheerful glow warmed our skin and kept the cold of winter at bay as we lay on the floor, sipped our Scotch, and talked of everything and nothing.

Throughout that winter I was a regular visitor to Holland, and when I was back home in Vancouver Lot kept the relationship alive with a constant stream of letters. Early one morning, some months after we first met, the phone rang in my Vancouver apartment. "Hi," said a tentative voice, "this is Lot." "How are you doing?" I replied, "how is . . ." She interrupted me, excited. "How would you feel if I came over for a visit?" "Great," I said, automatically assuming that she was talking several months into the future. "When do you have in mind?" "The day after tomorrow," she replied.

Lot occasionally had lunch with an old acquaintance who was fond of teasing her by asking: "When are you going to visit that friend of yours in Canada?" Finally he said it once too often. "Look, Kees, I'd love to go but I simply don't have the money—so for God's sake shut up." He stopped, taken aback, and after a moment said: "I'm sorry, you're absolutely right. Tell you what, I'll buy you a return ticket from Amsterdam to Vancouver right now, today, but on one condition—you have to go within forty-eight hours." Lot didn't believe he was serious, and said so. He was a good friend, but they had never had the type of relationship that would explain this level of generosity. Kees didn't even own a car, and when he didn't walk he normally cycled to his destination. "When my father died he left me quite a lot of money, much more than I really need," he explained, "and it's not often that you find yourself in a position to do something really nice for a friend. Do you want to go?" "Yes," said Lot, stunned. Kees bought the ticket.

Lot arrived in Vancouver the following day, and two weeks

later I flew back to Holland on an airline pass to settle her affairs—she had decided to stay in Canada. Six months later we were married at the town hall in The Hague, and the guest of honor was of course Kees. Our wedding party was held at Hathor. It closed for the occasion, but the similarity between our mix of wedding guests and its normal clientele was amazing, as someone uncharitably remarked. That was 25 years ago, and Lot and I have been together ever since.

2. The Challenge

A problem with dreams, at least those that involve boats and off-shore sailing, is that they tend to cost money and we didn't have any—or at least very little. The biggest challenge is not the voyage itself, but getting to the starting line with enough resources in terms of time and money to purchase a suitable boat and then set off. It seems to be a fact of life that people with the cash to easily buy a boat and finance an offshore cruise rarely have any interest in doing it, or lack the time—presumably because they are too busy making even more money—and the people who really want to do it may have the time but can't afford it.

Opinions as to what constitutes a suitable boat for offshore sailing are as varied as the people you ask. Successful crossings of both the Pacific and Atlantic have been completed in everything from row boats and rafts to open dinghies, but I can't say I was keen to emulate these achievements. An old guideline states that a yachtsman requires one foot of boat for every year of his life, but as I had precociously matured faster than my bank account this didn't seem to be an option either. Fortunately, in anything less than the most desperate offshore conditions size doesn't really matter. It's a vessel's strength and seaworthiness that count. The only major disadvantage of a smaller boat, other than lack of space, is that it tends to give a rougher ride but not necessarily a more dangerous one. The choice of any vessel involves a compromise of one sort or another, and so it was with an open mind that we began our exploration of the local used-boat market.

The results of our research were not encouraging. Depending on its age and condition, the type of boat we were interested in varied in price from 75,000 to 120,000 Canadian dollars and beyond; the sky's the limit when it comes to boat prices. A quick review of our assets revealed that in addition to CALLIOPE and a small three-year-old car, our total worth amounted to about $3,000 in savings. "I don't think we're going to be sailing any day soon," said Lot, with mild understatement. "Do you want to give up the idea?" I replied. "No," she said.

Hong Kong

I believe that we are the architects of our own fortune, but fate does seem to have a habit of intervening to help us achieve those things to which we have demonstrated, at least to ourselves, a burning commitment. So if fate played a role in bringing about our move to Hong Kong, then we must thank it for finally making our dream of ocean sailing possible.

I was attending a travel-industry trade fair in Winnipeg when I heard that a friend, who worked for the airline in Hong Kong, was being transferred. "Who's taking over from Dave?" I asked his boss, who was also attending the fair. "I don't know yet," said Harry, "anyone you'd recommend?" "Yes," I said, "me. It would be a great way to save money." "Nobody saves money in Hong Kong," Harry replied. "We will," I said. I got the job.

To move from Vancouver to Hong Kong is to exchange one of the world's most beautiful cities for one of the most exciting. On our arrival, in the summer of 1987, Hong Kong was a powerhouse teeming with people and energy. Its sole reason for being was to make money, and in this it had succeeded brilliantly. In less than a generation its industrious population had turned this centuries' old haunt of pirates into one of the world's leading economic powerhouses. With a flat tax rate of just over 15% it was understandably a haven for entrepreneurs of all kinds, and the government wisely benefited from the fact that 15% of a fortune is an infinitely greater sum than 30% of very little. Casting a shadow over this success was the uncertainty surrounding Hong Kong's return to China in 1997, and the impact this would have on its lifestyle. But rather than slow the pace of business activity, it seemed to increase it to a fever pitch as people saw the possibility of time running out on the road to wealth.

Cantonese, like all tonal languages, is very difficult for foreigners to master; the wrong accent means the wrong word. But Lot—like many of her countrymen—is fluent in English, French and German as well as in her mother tongue, and was determined to do her best to add Cantonese to the list. Armed with a Sony Walkman and a set of Cantonese language tapes, she spent hours studying the language and enjoyed practicing her new skills with the locals. One afternoon she set off to buy bones in the local market for our dog, Pretzel.

The forbidding concrete edifice which houses the central market in Hong Kong caters exclusively to the local population—it is not for the casual tourist or the faint of heart. Lot arrived late, just as it was closing, and entered by a side door. Inside, it was dark and gloomy as she picked her way towards the stairwell, avoiding the crates of live chickens and boxes of dead fish that littered the floor. Climbing the stairs she passed the remains of the vegetable market on the second floor, and continued up to the meat department on top of the three-story building.

The entire floor was divided into small cubicles, each illuminated by a dim naked lightbulb that hung on a long cord from the high ceiling. Only two cubicles remained open, and she approached the closest while reciting in her head the Cantonese words that she had been practicing. "Nay yau mo kwat maai?" she asked the man behind the counter. He stared at her indifferently and made no reply. She tried again, this time tapping her arm for emphasis, "Nay yau mo kwat maai (Do you have any bones)?" The man's lack of interest was palpable, and she was getting nowhere. She turned to the next booth—her last chance. "Nay yau mo kwat maai?" she tried again desperately. Again no response, and then suddenly the eyes of a young assistant standing quietly in the background lit up, and he dove towards a large wicker basket from which protruded a huge pair of horns. He grabbed them and pulled.

They emerged attached to an enormous skinned cow's head, minus eyes and lower jaw, which he put down on the counter with an ominous grinding noise as its upper teeth scraped along the cement surface. Lot swallowed, and tried to look encouraging while getting across the message that he was on the right track but this wasn't exactly what she had in mind. The young assistant, determined to satisfy whatever strange compulsion was driving this crazy gweipo (female foreign devil), dove back into the basket and emerged with a three-foot femur that must have come from a buffalo. Lot nodded enthusiastically, indicating that they were getting closer, but gestured that this was still a bit bigger than she had in mind. He explored his gory basket yet again, and returned with a lower foreleg with most of its meat trimmed off but its hoof still attached. With an expectant expression on his young face he held his trophy high in the air, its macabre hoof dangling, as Lot gave him a thumbs up sign. Encouraged, he disappeared and returned moments later with all four of the animal's skinned lower legs, complete with hooves. Lot now had all four legs, hooves, and the skinned upper skull, and it began to look as if the conversation continued she would soon be able to reassemble the whole cow into a bovine recreation that would warm the heart of Frankenstein. To everyone's satisfaction a compromise was reached. Lot paid the requested reasonable price and quickly left with her prize— two front legs minus their hooves!

Forty miles west of Hong Kong, on the opposite shore of the Pearl River Delta, lies the ancient port city of Macao. For centuries it was a Portuguese colony but, like Hong Kong itself, it has recently reverted back to Chinese rule. Served by a regular high-speed hydroplane service, Macao was a favorite weekend getaway destination for residents of Hong Kong wanting to escape the pressure of business for a few days. Before it was renovated into something more lavish, a favorite destination for the younger crowd was the old Bela Vista hotel. Its attraction was its low cost, turn-of-the-century gilded decor, and an aura from its rich and colorful past that hinted of the disreputable. The interesting stains that covered the red carpets and pink wallpaper in its rooms were sensibly never removed by the management, who perhaps recognized them for what they were—statements of character. "Every stain could tell a story," a friend succinctly observed. However he also claimed, though I have my doubts, that he once entered a room and hung his coat on what he thought was a hook on the wall, only to discover a few moments later, when it fell off, that it was a mushroom. He swears it's true, but Jon was always prone to take a good story a bit far. Macao is also famous for its endlessly depressing casino—which, after one exploratory visit, we always made a point of avoiding.

Macao is the destination of one of the biggest sailing events of the year in Hong Kong—the annual Macao Layover Race. We set off early one morning on a friend's boat, JACARANDA, and as I had been nominated as navigator, I suppose I was largely to blame for what was to follow. The tricky thing about rivers is that they flow—they have a current that can vary in speed depending on the position of sandbars and shallows. This is not normally a problem when crossing the Pearl because it is well marked with buoys, as long as you can see them! But fog started rolling in when we were less than halfway across and it became progressively thicker. An hour after running into the first patches we were in a pea soup, and without radar or any other electronic navigation equipment we were reduced to dead reckoning. The compass gave us a good sense of direction, but the problem for the helmsman was in knowing how much to allow for the drift caused by the variable current. As darkness fell we continued feeling our way slowly westward, until out of the gloom loomed the dark silhouette of a row of pilings and a floating dock that appeared to be some sort of coal terminal. We decided that discretion was the better part of nautical valor and tied up to wait it out until the fog cleared.

There were ten of us on board and as we were always willing to make the most of any situation we decided it was party time, so once the boat was secure we broke out the grog. After a while, someone came up with the idea of playing charades, and the party went from strength to strength. At one o'clock in the morning the piercing searchlight of a Macao police boat rudely interrupted our revelry. The fog was still dense, and we discovered later that over half the racing fleet of more than 100 boats was scattered, like us, along a 20-mile strip on the western shore of the delta. "Follow us," commanded the voice over the megaphone. "Go awaysh," was the immediate reply from one of the happier members of our crew, "we don't wansh to be reshcued." But our liberators were in no mood to argue, and we joined the line of boats that the police were leading into Macao—like a mother duck with her chicks in tow.

Once in harbor the party continued, and my last recollection of that night is standing on the back of our boat with a fellow Canadian, giving a rousing rendition of *Oh Canada* to an audience who showed their hearty appreciation by releasing some of their valuable emergency flares in our direction, several of which actually hit their mark. The next morning the Macao police were understanding. Before leaving we asked if we could buy diesel fuel. "No," was the firm reply, "but we'd be happy to give you some." I think they would have done anything just to see the back of us. Ah, a great place Macao!

3. *Moonshiner*

Canadian Airlines, like most other carriers in the late 1980s, was losing money and began to lay off staff. So I suppose I should have been relieved when my boss phoned one morning with some unexpected news. "Head office wants to know if you would be interested in moving to New Zealand as General Manager. Congratulations, it's a fantastic opportunity." Any sensible yuppie would have jumped at the opportunity, but I guess I just wasn't the sensible type. "Well . . . I'm not sure, Harry. Let me think about it and talk it over with Lot." He was astounded at my lack of enthusiasm and urged me to accept, before I made what he correctly foresaw as a self-destructive career move.

We decided to reject the offer thinking, naïvely, that we could continue in Hong Kong as before. I asked Harry to pass on my "thanks but no thanks" reply and assumed a low profile. It didn't work. A couple of days later Harry called back. "Head office isn't happy, to put it mildly," he said. "They say that because you've turned down New Zealand, you can't stay in Hong Kong." Then the axe fell: "They want to transfer you back to Calgary." Now I know Calgary is a marvelous place. Some of my best friends (well, one of them) live in Calgary. It's a wonderful area for cows, cowboys, ranching, and oil. It has beautiful scenery, a great social and cultural life, the magnificent Rocky Mountains, superb skiing, and the people are warm and friendly. There's only one problem—it doesn't have an ocean. I drafted my resignation letter the next day, and a few weeks later I left the company where I had worked for sixteen years.

There were two immediate consequences: we had nowhere to live, and I had no job. Finding accommodation at an afford-able price was next to impossible in Hong Kong, but I suddenly had an idea. "Why don't we buy a boat now, and live on it?" I suggested to Lot. "Do we have enough money?" she asked. A key element of our savings plan had been to avoid borrowing and paying interest, so taking out a loan to buy a boat was something we needed to avoid. "It depends on how long it takes me to find a job," I replied. "If we don't have to dig into our savings to cover our living expenses, we might just be able to afford it." So once again we began visiting yacht brokers, while I simultaneously looked for work.

The job problem was solved first, when I was hired a few weeks later by a Hong Kong consulting company as project manager for a contract they had just signed with a major US air-line. Shortly afterwards we received a call from one of the local brokers: "I think we've found something that might interest you, come and take a look." "What is it, and how big is it?" I asked. "It's a 37-foot steel ketch," said the agent, Barbara. "It just ar-rived from the Philippines with a family of Australians on board. It seems they want to stay in Hong Kong and are interested in selling." "We're on our way," I replied. "Oh, there's just one thing," she interrupted before I could hang up, "it doesn't have a head—there's no toilet—but I've told them that if they hope to sell it they'd better install one and they're working on it." "How did they survive without one?" I wondered aloud. "Heaven knows—'buckit and chuckit', I guess," said Barbara.

It was the fall of 1990, and with or without a head we fell in love with MOONSHINER as soon as we saw her. She was a hard chine steel ketch, built in Australia in 1978 by her owner, Paul, to a Dufour design. He soon discovered she was underpowered, and added a three-foot bowsprit to increase her sail area, which brought her overall length up to 40 feet. She was narrow in the beam at only 11' 3", and had a moderate keel with a cut-away forefoot and a skeg-hung rudder. After a surveyor gave her an enthusiastic thumbs up, we agreed to buy her, subject to Paul completing the job of installing the head. A few days later I called the broker to see how things were going. Barbara started to laugh. "There's been a bit of a hitch," she admitted. "I just visited the boat and Paul is halfway through installing the toilet bowl at the end of the bed." The bed occupied almost the entire rear cabin, with only a small area left over for dressing in front of the "pillow" end. This was where Paul had decided to install his plumbing. The offending porcelain was soon removed to a more appropriate location and a few days later we moved aboard.

Aberdeen Marina

Among the many incongruities that Hong Kong has inherited from its colonial past are place names that seem totally inappropriate; nothing could be less Scottish than the village of Aberdeen. Located on the south shore of Hong Kong Island, Aberdeen is famous for its gaudy, multi-story floating restaurants that have become a mandatory stop for busloads of tourists seeking an authentic Chinese experience. But long before the first tourist arrived, Aberdeen's protected harbor was home to hundreds of seaworthy wooden fishing junks and the people who lived and worked on them. Each boat sheltered three or more generations of the same family and everyone, from the very old to the very young, had their place and responsibilities. Today, although the boats are still there, many of the fishing families have been re-housed in sterile high-rise buildings that dominate the waterfront. But it is still a community whose heart beats to the rhythm of the sea; sampans pursue their trade like busy water beetles, chandlers and marine stores line the narrow streets, fishermen repair their nets and dry their fish on the bustling waterfront while their children swim, apparently immune, in the polluted water of the inner harbor. Nearby lies Aberdeen Marina, which was to be our home for the next two years.

Our live-aboard community consisted of doctors, airline pilots, engineers, businessmen and journalists who, in addition to their love of boats and the sea, shared one other characteristic in common—they were all party animals. The marina had developed its own social etiquette to cope with the lack of privacy; if people were below deck you generally didn't disturb them, but if anyone was sitting in the cockpit this was taken as an automatic invitation to a party—teetotalism was rare amongst our neighbors. Fortune often favored the foolish amongst the marina's larger than life and colorful characters—such as the time a rotund journalist friend, after consuming more than his usual quantity of liquid nourishment, woke up in the middle of the night to find himself floating on his back between the marina floats. The occupants of the closest boat were summoned by a thumping on the hull and a request to "pull me out of this !!**!! water." Why he didn't drown no one ever knew.

On another occasion, perhaps re-living his days as a Green Beret (yes, really), the same neighbor was demonstrating how to conceal a 9mm automatic pistol in the back of his belt when it suddenly fell into his nether regions. The owner of the gun, for whose benefit the demonstration was being given, had taken legal delivery of the weapon that afternoon and was sailing for the Philippines early the next morning. As our hero groped for the offending weapon in his makeshift fruit of the loom Y-front holster, the rest of the guests backed away in tears of laughter; nobody seemed to know if the gun was loaded.

Guns

Whether or not to carry guns is a fundamental question for any small boat planning a cruise in Southeast Asia. The region has the highest incidence of piracy in the world, and shotguns or pistols are seen by some people as essential for self-defense if they are unlucky enough to be attacked. In our experience, the decision is usually resolved according to a boat's nationality; American boats frequently carry guns but other nationalities normally don't. An exception to this rule was a young American singlehander from Detroit, whom we met while he was visiting Hong Kong in the middle of his second circumnavigation. After going around the first time in his small, 30-foot, wooden sloop he must have decided he needed a bigger challenge, because he had removed his engine and set out to repeat the feat under sail alone.

He had found temporary work as a rigger and boat painter in Aberdeen, and I asked his advice about carrying guns because I knew he'd done a lot of sailing in Asia. "Don't buy a gun unless you know you can kill somebody with it," was his advice. "Every boat you're likely to meet between here and Thailand, including fishing boats, carry AK 47s on board—lots of them—and they are a lot less squeamish about using them than you would be. And whatever you do, don't bring out a gun unless you're about to use it. Life is a lot cheaper for any 'bad guys' you're likely to meet than it probably is for you, and showing off your gun won't deter them, it'll just up the ante and force a confrontation. My advice is don't take them. If you're unlucky enough to get boarded just give them what they want. When you do that, they rarely harm anyone."

We took his advice and were glad we did; we didn't know it yet, but MOONSHINER would face two potential pirate attacks before we left Asia, and the fact that we didn't have guns onboard worked in our favor. Almost all the fatalities during pirate attacks on small boats—at least when survivors have been left to tell the tale—have taken place when the victim has brandished or fired a weapon.

4. The San Fernando Race

As the boat drove through the night towards the south, a brilliant full moon lay directly ahead, illuminating a spectacular and angry ocean. Ragged clouds tore across the sky, casting fleeting shadows on the moon's reflection in the water; a shimmering silver road beckoned from the bow to the horizon and pointed the way towards our destination in the Philippines. Spray exploded into the air as the boat attacked each wave, only to be whipped by the gale high above the cockpit until it rejoined the ocean far to leeward. It was just after midnight and the wind, which had started to build the previous afternoon, was gusting to 45 knots and still increasing. Without warning the vessel heeled, and solid water cascaded over the deck as the wheel spun uselessly in the helmsman's hand. The steering cable had parted. We didn't know it yet, but this was only the first round in a fight that would escalate as the night wore on—a fight against conditions the boat was never designed to handle. Less than two hours later, with the wind still increasing, the boom of the 55-foot sloop tore itself off the mast. We were participating in the San Fernando Yacht Race and the situation was rapidly getting out of control.

The events that led to that memorable night began months earlier while we were returning to Hong Kong on the second leg of the Macao layover race. The morning after the marine police towed us into Macao we awoke to find that the fog had cleared—at least the external fog; the fog induced by too much partying took longer to dissipate. But the weather was kind and we convalesced while enjoying a slow sail home under mostly sunny skies. The only excitement came when JACARANDA's steering cable snapped, but in the light conditions it didn't take long to fix, and in less than half an hour we were underway again. With the benefit of hindsight we made a serious mistake by not thinking *why* the cable had parted. If we had, we would have saved ourselves a lot of grief later. Anyway, it was on this return trip that Steve, our captain, suggested that we enter JACARANDA in the next San Fernando Race.

The 600-mile race across the South China Sea from Hong Kong to San Fernando—on the Philippine island of Luzon—is one of the most famous regattas in Asia, and the opportunity to participate was too good to miss. Our crew hailed from Australia, Holland, Canada, Germany, England, Switzerland and South Africa. Most of us had sailed for many years, and we often spent weekends together cruising the waters around Hong Kong. With a large boat, and a crew of ten reasonably seasoned sailors to share the work, I thought we could look forward to a safe and comfortable passage, but I hadn't reckoned with the power of the South China Sea.

On the eve of the big race the weather forecast was mixed. A disturbance was slowly approaching from the north, but as our course lay to the southeast most of the fleet was expected to stay ahead of the worst weather. As it turned out, this was only true for the fastest leading boats—such as the world-class ocean racer ROTHMANS, which disappeared over the horizon so quickly that the rest of the fleet almost forgot that it was participating. It completed the course in a little over two days and by the time anybody else arrived at the finish line it was long gone.

For three days we sailed in light winds under a flat sky that was dominated by bands of translucent clouds that partially obscured the sun, and were tinged with strange shades of pink and green. I felt uneasy. It was as if the weather couldn't decide what to do. Was it going to clear up and let the normal monsoon winds speed us on our way? Or was it contemplating throwing something more sinister in our direction? One way or the other we would soon find out. Meanwhile, the daily radio updates indicated little change to the original forecast—most boats were still expected to stay ahead of the area of strongest winds. By the morning of the fourth day we were well beyond the dangerously shallow coastal plateau, and the threat of the short steep seas for which it is notorious. Sailing in deep water, and with the northwest coast of the Philippines only 100 miles ahead, we thought we were in the clear. But just before noon, the wind started to build.

The first hint of trouble came when we discovered that the hull was flexing so much in the building seas that the cabin doors couldn't be closed. Weeks earlier I'd noticed small cracks radiating outward from the corner of JACARANDA's door and window frames, and pointed them out to Steve. He thought they were just a cosmetic problem, a minor flaw in the fiber-glass cabin liner and unrelated to the hull itself. But now I wasn't so sure. I began to suspect that his beautiful Taiwanese-built yacht wasn't strong enough to face hard offshore condi-tions. I tried to put the idea out of my mind—it was too late to worry about it anyway—and concentrate on other things, in-cluding not screwing up the navigation.

Throughout the afternoon the wind grew stronger, and by four o'clock it was blowing a full gale. At dusk the sky began to clear, and soon after sunset a full moon rose out of the angry sea to keep us company. For the next few hours the conditions got progressively worse, and by midnight the waves, at least to my inexperienced eyes, were becoming enormous. In fact they no longer qualified as *waves* in any sense that I understood the word. They were huge flat-sided slabs of water that towered over us in the troughs, and moments later raised us up to offer a mountaineer's view of row upon row of glistening silver peaks and cascading foam. Then all hell broke loose.

JACARANDA suddenly broached wildly, lying for a second with the mast almost in the sea as silver water broke over the deck. Everyone in the cockpit was wearing a safety harness, but we instinctively grabbed the nearest solid object, and hung on for dear life. "We've lost the bloody steering again," Steve yelled above the noise and the mayhem; the staccato whiplash of crazily flogging sails added to the howl of the wind as the boat bucked and rolled helplessly. After a few seconds she began to recover, and slowly settled herself to lie sideways to the waves, drifting downwind.

Canadian Bob and another member of the crew disappeared into the bowels of the boat to check out the problem, while the rest of us sorted out the mess of lines on deck and waited. Then Steve, with his usual gung-ho enthusiasm, said "Let's use the autopilot. It's connected directly to the rudder and we can keep on racing while they fix the wheel. It'll drain the battery pretty fast, but we can run the engine—as long as we keep it in neutral it's not against the race rules." By this time the idea of racing wasn't at the top of my agenda—if Scottie could have beamed me ashore at that moment I would have been eternally grateful. But it did seem a good idea to get control of the boat back as quickly as possible, so I was all in favor.

Steve tried to start the engine, but the expected roar of the diesel failed to materialize. "I can't get the damn thing in neutral, so it won't start," he announced. "There must be something dragging on the propeller." A safety feature on the engine neutralized the starter motor unless it was in neutral, but we had earlier put the gearbox into reverse to stop the prop shaft from turning. We looked over the side. Sure enough, we could see a line disappearing under the hull that must have formed a bight, or loop, around the propeller. In the strong wind, the drift of the boat created a drag on the line that prevented the gearbox from being put back into neutral. No neutral meant no engine, and so the only alternative was to remain hove-to until the repairs were finished. This awful job took our stalwart volunteers 45 minutes, working head down in the bilge of the heaving boat. Despite the violent motion, adrenaline kept their seasickness at bay until the work was finished—when they both rushed headlong to the rail.

After they recovered they told us that the cable had broken in exactly the same place as on our return from Macao: at a point where it passed over one of the steering sheaves—the pulleys that lead the cable from the wheel to the rudder. They were simply too small for the job and the back and forth flexing of the cable, as it rolled over them, had eventually stressed it to the breaking point. If we'd paid more attention the first time it happened, we could have solved the problem by installing fittings of the correct size. But thoughts of "would-a, could-a, should-a," as a sailing friend is fond of saying, get you nowhere.

As we got underway again the wind showed no sign of abating. The big mainsail had three sets of reef points—to enable the crew to reduce its size in a blow—but only the first two points had permanent reefing lines attached, and so there was no easy way to pull down the third reef, which was now urgently required. Two days earlier we'd passed a peaceful afternoon debating the wisdom of permanently attaching a third line. The majority of the crew decided that it wasn't required—that in the unlikely event that conditions were ever bad enough to warrant three reefs, a spare line could be attached at that time. What seemed like a reasonable argument in daylight, relaxing in a 12-knot breeze, lost its appeal in the middle of the night with a huge sea running and the wind gusting well over 40 knots. So the mainsheet was eased to luff the sail—spilling some of the wind.

JACARANDA surged through the night towards Luzon under a scrap of foresail and two reefs in her luffing main. I took the helm for an hour with a mixture of exhilaration and fear, but the boat seemed well balanced, without too much pressure on the wheel, and I began to relax. Most of the spray was passing clear over the boat, leaving the cockpit relatively dry and I was actually starting to enjoy the experience when something hit me hard on the head. At first I thought that a sheet must have broken loose, but I looked down to see a heavyweight flying fish, well over a foot long, flopping helplessly in the cockpit at my feet. Everyone thought this was hilarious, and as soon as they stopped laughing the poor fish was quickly returned to the ocean. No doubt it was as surprised as I was by the experience.

* * *

Perhaps the luffing sail placed an unusual strain on the gooseneck fitting, which connected the boom to the mast. Or maybe the fitting itself had long contained some undetected flaw, patiently waiting to reveal itself at the right moment. Whatever the reason, less than two hours after repairing the steering there was a loud crash, and without warning the big boom suddenly tore itself off the mast. The three-quarter inch stainless steel gooseneck plate had ripped apart as if it was made of paper. For a moment we all froze, in shock. As we slowly came to our senses and took in the situation, we saw that the loose boom hadn't been blown downwind, where it would almost certainly have ripped the sail. Instead, it was flailing wildly on the windward side of the mast and threatening to impale anyone who came within range. I grabbed a line and crawled forward along the heaving deck with another crewmember. After a memorable struggle, in which my partner received a nasty flesh wound from the sharp edge of the broken fitting, we eventually managed to subdue it and lashed it back in place with the sail miraculously still intact.

"What's going to break next?" one of the crew wondered aloud. To reduce the strain on the boat we decided to reduce our small area of headsail even further. But the furling gear gave more resistance than usual. "We've lost the damned halyard," someone shouted, and we looked up to see that he was right—it had chafed through just below the masthead. Without a halyard to hold up the sail, only the strength of the wind, and the fact that most of the sail was already furled around the forestay, kept it from falling to the deck. We managed to give it a couple more turns for good measure, and then sat watching the awesome beauty of that wild moonlit night as we waited for the dawn, fervently hoping the gale would soon be over.

Fear

Perhaps the most frequent question non-sailors ask when they hear we have crossed oceans in a small boat is "Do you sail at night or do you anchor?" The second most common question is "Don't you get afraid?" The first question is easy. In 18,000 feet of water—over three miles—our 250 feet of anchor chain has trouble reaching the bottom. The second question is more difficult, because sometimes—though thankfully not too often—I do.

Anyone who sets out to cross an ocean in a small boat without feeling a certain amount of apprehension is either a fool, or ignorant of what they're getting into. A healthy dose of respect for the sea, and what it can do, is the beginning of good seamanship, and this kind of tempered fear is a sailor's friend. But at the other extreme, fear, if it leads to panic, can paralyze a crew or lead to irrational decisions. And a low level of fear, if it persists in non-threatening conditions, can destroy the pleasure of the experience. We became friendly with the wife of a retired Merchant Marine captain, who was circumnavigating with her husband. She admitted, in his absence, that, "I never really enjoy sailing because I always feel afraid."

Fortunately, the reaction of the captain's wife seems to be rare, and most of our cruising friends thoroughly enjoy their offshore adventures. Careful planning can eliminate most hair-raising experiences at sea, but not all of them, and nobody knows how they will react when the going gets tough until they have actually experienced it. Most sailors who have been caught out in severe weather report being too busy taking care of the situation to really think about being afraid. Eric Hiscock, one of the great pioneers of ocean cruising whose books have inspired thousands to follow in his wake, quoted R. L. Stevenson on the subject: *"It is commonplace that we cannot answer for ourselves until we have been tried. But it is not so common a reflection, and surely more consoling, that we usually find ourselves a great deal better and braver than we thought . . . good in a man's spirit will not suffer itself to be overlaid and rarely or never deserts him in the hour of need."*

On the few occasions when Lot and I subsequently ran into bad weather aboard MOONSHINER I seemed to don a pair of mental blinkers that focused my attention on the problem at hand and excluded anything beyond. If the wind blew at 30 knots I concentrated on what I would do if it blew 35. When it did, I started planning what action to take if it reached 40 or more. But the most light-hearted and effective secret that Lot and I have developed for handling stressful situations is our agreement—*not to have our nervous breakdowns on the same day.* It works. If she senses I'm getting stressed out, then a helpful reminder that "You freaked out yesterday. Today it's my turn," soon puts most problems back into perspective.

Dawn broke in an almost cloudless sky, with the wind still blowing at over 40 knots. By now we were conditioned to expect the worst, and I began looking around the boat—trying to anticipate what might break next. The roller furling line caught my eye. If it failed, the entire foresail, unsupported because of the broken halyard, would immediately unfurl and we would have another major problem on our hands. "Let's attach a lazy furling line with a rolling hitch," I suggested. "If the original chafes through we'd still have something to stop the sail from unwinding." The only problem was that I couldn't remember how to tie a rolling hitch. So I went below and tore a photograph of the knot out of a cruising manual, and we took it with us as we crawled along the deck towards the bow. Whether or not it would have held if the original line had broken is a moot point, but at least we were now thinking in terms of prevention rather than how to react after the fact.

Later that morning, our fifth day at sea, the wind began to moderate. It was soon decreasing even quicker than it had built the previous afternoon, and within a few hours it had fallen to less than ten knots. In a final irony, it took us well over an hour to complete the last two miles of the course, with only a breath of wind left to push us into the protected bay and across the finish line. As we gratefully dropped anchor, the boat, with her sagging sails, broken halyard, wrecked boom, and a trailing line that was caught around the propeller, looked as if she had been on the losing side at the battle of Trafalgar.

The party held ashore to celebrate the end of the race was

wild; a crewmember from a competing boat, that had also taken a beating in the gale, captured the spirit of the occasion when she observed, "We're all celebrating the fact that we're still alive." As if to prove how fickle the weather can be, on our return trip to Hong Kong a few days later we had no wind whatsoever; we powered the whole way over a glassy calm sea and passed the time reading and soaking up the sun. It was hard to believe it was the same stretch of ocean that we'd crossed only a few days before. "Do you still want to leave next year on MOONSHINER?" I asked Lot after we arrived safely back home. "Of course," she replied.

5. Fluke

Fluke came into our lives one hot August morning, just after we'd quit our jobs to work full time on preparing MOONSHINER for the long journey to Europe via Singapore, Sri Lanka, and the Red Sea. Our plan was to spend several years in Holland, replenishing our cruising funds, before continuing our homeward voyage to Vancouver via the Atlantic and the Panama Canal. It had been more than seven years since we first set ourselves the goal of ocean sailing, and our dream was finally within sight.

We were sitting on deck deciding which job to tackle next, when Lot called out, "Who's your new friend?" I looked up to see one of our neighbors walking along the float, followed by the saddest and most bedraggled looking dog you could imagine. Obviously starving, the animal was barely able to walk. As they got closer we could see its ribs showing starkly under the skin. Heaven knows when it had last eaten. "Are you going to keep it?" asked Lot. "No way," was the reply. "I pulled it out of the water a couple of minutes ago and it's been following me ever since." Both Lot and I badly missed our old dog, Pretzel, who had died a few months earlier. One more look and Lot's mind was made up, "Hang on, let's see if we have something for it to eat."

She went below and reappeared with a carton of eggs. "I guess it's not really dog food, but at the moment it's the best we have," she said as she cracked six of them into a bowl while the animal's eyes grew large in anticipation. It pounced on the unexpected feast, and the bowl and contents were about to go flying. Without thinking, Lot reached out and took the bowl away from the starving animal to move it to a safer location. The dog's only reaction was to pause in surprise, look wistfully at her, and then gently give her hand a lick as she replaced the food.

At that moment I think we both knew that the dog had found herself a new home. However, her status as a full member of the family wasn't confirmed until a few days later when we decided we should give her a name. "Any ideas?" I asked Lot. She replied, "If she'd arrived a few days sooner we would have missed her because we'd still have been at work—it's just a fluke she chose the moment she did." "Well, anchors have flukes, and whales too," I said, and so "Fluke" she became.

Fluke was only about eighteen months old when we found her, and with care and good food her condition soon improved. But even though she was growing stronger, and we suspected she was no stranger to life on the water, we were concerned about how she would adapt to a long ocean passage on a small boat. We discussed Fluke's options with our vet. "If you look after her, she'll be better off sailing with you than if we try to put her up for adoption in Hong Kong, and there's no guarantee anybody else will take her," he advised. We agreed, but as an extra precaution we tied safety netting to MOONSHINER's lifelines to help keep her on deck, and later we made her a safety harness so we could keep her securely attached to the boat while we were underway. As it turned out, Fluke took to life on the ocean as if she was born to it, which I guess she was.

A few weeks later we took a break in our preparations to visit our families back in Europe, and made arrangements to leave Fluke with a friend in Hong Kong during our absence. We were afraid that when she found herself in another new and unfamiliar environment she might be tempted to wander off and come looking for us, and so we took the precaution of attaching the phone number of our friend Keith to her collar.

Sure enough, several days after we left, Fluke went missing during the night—just as we'd feared. Fortunately, someone spotted her wandering the waterfront and handed her over to the police. But as they had no immediate luck contacting Keith, and there were no animal shelters in the vicinity, the police were faced with the problem of what to do with her. Someone came to the conclusion that any canine found wandering the streets of Hong Kong in the middle of the night must be of doubtful character. So the police left her with the guard at the main gate of the nearby jail in the village of Stanley, Hong Kong's most notorious maximum-security facility.

The prison officials made contact with Keith the next day. Fluke was granted parole and released into his custody, but only after it was made clear that he should be ashamed for the state of near starvation of the animal. "But it's not even my dog," he protested. "Then why are you picking it up?" After a quick explanation, Fluke and her rescuer beat a hasty retreat. Fluke was not yet two years old and already a jailbird!

Preparation

Although MOONSHINER had been well built and maintained, after 13 years of cruising full-time in the Pacific she needed an extensive refit. We were about to learn just how frustrating and discouraging this process can be—everything seemed to cost twice as much and take twice as long as we had anticipated. And to make matters worse, we compounded the problem by quitting our jobs too soon to work full time on the boat. It's easy to be wise after the fact, but it would have made more sense for one of us to keep working, and then we'd have had at least one income to cover the long list of unforeseen expenses. It's amazing how fast the bank account goes down once your income stops.

Our costs were considerably higher than they would have been in Europe or North America because the few chandlers selling yachting gear in Hong Kong had little competition, and marked up their prices accordingly. We imported big-ticket items from either England or the US, but it was the high price of many small items purchased locally that "nickel and dimed" us to death. We shipped a 60 lb. CQR anchor and 300 feet of chain from London for considerably less money than our local chandler wanted to charge. But although equipment was expensive in Hong Kong, labor was relatively cheap and we took advantage of this to get worn seats re-upholstered and woodwork repaired at very reasonable cost.

During the final fitting out, we decided it made no sense to keep paying the high charges in our marina and we began looking for somewhere cheaper to moor MOONSHINER. We moved first to a buoy in Aberdeen Harbour and then later, when the boat needed hauling out of the water, we found a less expensive marina, well out of town, where we could quietly complete the work.

It was at the mooring buoy that Fluke decided to take her revenge on the Hong Kong police department that she probably still blamed for her imprisonment. We were not on board when it happened, but we got a full account from an amused neighbor, Graeme, who was moored next to us. Two Hong Kong harbor policemen were making a routine night patrol of the anchorage when they came alongside MOONSHINER in their boat. They tapped on the hull to see if anyone was at home, and when they got no reply they decided to come aboard and check things out. Meanwhile Fluke, who was sleeping quietly on deck, woke up and suddenly appeared from behind the mast just as Hong Kong's finest climbed over the gunnels. To their mutual surprise they suddenly came eye to eye. Fluke gave a yelp of terror and leaped back into the security of the cockpit while the policemen, equally startled, simultaneously made a dive back into the police launch, gunned the engine and took off. We never heard from the police again; if they were still keeping an eye on the boat it was from a very safe distance.

Ancient Land—Ancient Waters

During our last months in Hong Kong, whenever I needed to take a break and get away from MOONSHINER for a few hours, I would take Fluke and together we would climb a hill behind the marina. The exposed summit was usually windy and deserted, and while Fluke ran through the grass I would sit and admire the view. Beneath us lay the familiar village of Aberdeen with its hundreds of anchored fishing junks, narrow twisting streets, and white high-rise buildings lining the waterfront. To the west, beyond Hong Kong Island, lay the estuary of the mighty Pearl River. And to the south, in the distance, I could see the offshore islands that belonged to China and beyond them, stretching blue and silent to the horizon, lay the South China Sea. I was looking at one of the oldest trading routes in the world, and for centuries the nearby city of Guangzhou, on the Pearl River, had been one of its major hubs.

As long ago as the seventh century, China was a melting pot of cultures as traders arrived with goods from Indonesia, Burma, East Africa, Persia and beyond. In return, China traded silk and porcelain. The silk was transported via the legendary overland Silk Route through Central Asia and on to the Middle East and Europe. Individual traders didn't make the whole journey, but they transported the goods in relays. The porcelain trade was based on a 5,000-mile sea route that stretched from Guangzhou to the spice ports of Sumatra and Malaya, and on to Oman and the Persian Gulf via Ceylon and India. In the early years Arab seafarers controlled the business, and the legends of Sinbad-the-Sailor probably date from this period. As many as 200,000 foreigners—Arabs, Persians, Indians and Malays— were already living in Guangzhou 1,300 years ago, as traders and artisans.

China began developing a navy during the Song dynasty (960-1290) and towards the end of this period the effort was accelerated by mounting fears of a Mongol invasion. Their fears were justified. The Mongols were originally a group of disunited and obscure tribes living in the outer regions of the Gobi Desert in Central Asia. They were united in the twelfth century under the brilliant and savage leadership of Genghis Khan who, with a relatively small army of just over 100,000 men fighting on horseback, conquered most of continental Asia and was soon knocking on the back door of Europe. His tactics were brutal and effective. If a town fought back he would lay siege to it, and once it was captured he would exterminate the inhabitants. Not surprisingly, towns began to surrender as soon as they heard that Genghis and his merry men were in their vicinity.

By the time of his death in 1227, Genghis Khan's armies had successfully invaded China and captured the northern city of Beijing, and over the next 15 years they went on to conquer all of northern China. In 1264 Kublai Khan, a grandson of Genghis Khan, relocated his capital from Mongolia to Beijing. He built a magnificent palace for himself—the Forbidden City—and in 1271 he established the dynastic name Yuan. The Mongols soon conquered the rest of China, which for the next 100 years became essentially an occupied country. At its height, the Mongol empire extended from Siberia to the Arabian Peninsula, and from Poland to my hill overlooking Aberdeen Harbour.

6. Leaving Hong Kong

Heading over the horizon for the first time, towards a land-fall hundreds of miles away, is an intimidating prospect. So when we heard that an informal sailing race was leaving Hong Kong bound for the Philippine resort of Puerto Galera in early April, we decided to join it for the first leg of our journey. At the pre-race meeting I discovered I was surrounded by soul mates. "I propose that when we get to Pratas Reef we can stop to fish without incurring a penalty," said one of the skippers to loud applause. So the race rules were amended, and each participant was allowed to deduct the hours spent fishing from his or her elapsed time. To make watch keeping easier, and reduce the workload while we were still gaining our sea legs, we invited Keith and his friend Vanessa to accompany us.

Memories of the morning of our departure remain a blur, as we rushed madly through our final checklist and made sure everything was aboard. But finally, to the sound of air-horns and the cheers of our neighbors, we motored out of the harbor and into the China Sea. Our great adventure was about to begin.

The sea and the sky were grey, and the wind blustery, as we watched the hills of Hong Kong disappear into the rain squalls as night began to fall. Earlier, just after the start of the race, a friend from the Aberdeen Marina caught up with us in his larger boat and waved a final farewell before jibing and heading back to the city that had been our home for almost five years. After dreaming of this day for so long I was surprised to feel a deep sadness, knowing that I was leaving behind people and places that had touched my life but I would never see again. There is a dark side to the gypsy life—caught between uncertainty and regret, where the horizon ahead is still unknown and the land behind draws us back.

What a difference a day makes. Next morning the off-watch crew awoke to a clear blue sky and moderate winds. We were now in deeper water, outside the shallow coastal shelf, and as a result the sea was much calmer: in shallow water, waves become steeper and higher as soon as they can "feel" the bottom and friction begins to slow them down. The sun glinted reassuringly off the sea, and we finally began to enjoy ourselves as the steady monsoon wind filled our sails and carried us south towards the tropics. Our dream was finally coming true, and we were beginning our journey by following in the wake of one of the greatest armadas ever to put to sea—the great Chinese Treasure Fleet.

China's Great Armada

In the early years of the fifteenth century the Treasure Fleet rode the monsoon winds of the South China Sea and the Indian Ocean carrying 30,000 sailors, soldiers, physicians, artisans, traders, ambassadors, interpreters and courtesans in up to 100 gargantuan ships, all under the command of the legendary eunuch, Admiral Zheng He. The great fleet sailed from China seven times over a period of 30 years. As a maritime force it was unstoppable. And yet a few short years after Zheng's final expedition his fleet ceased to exist—passing into oblivion as China turned inward and lost interest in naval expansion—its magnificent boats left to rot at their moorings.

Zheng's first voyage left Nanjing, on the Yangtze River, in 1405 with over 60 ships, including specialized boats for transporting grain, or water, or horses for the cavalry. The fleet also included warships, supply ships, and troop transports. The first expedition sailed with 28,000 men and made stops in Vietnam, Java, and Malacca before heading west across the Indian Ocean to Sri Lanka and on to Calicut and Cochin—major trading centers on the southwest coast of India. They remained in India until the spring of 1407, when they used the seasonal shift in the monsoon wind to sail back to China. On their way home they ran into a violent storm in the South China Sea, and the terrified crew believed they had encountered a dragon lurking in the ocean who churned the seas with his claws and spat spray and foam. The sailors appealed for their lives to Tianfei, the Celestial Consort, and their pleas were apparently answered when a lantern appeared in the rigging (presumably St. Elmo's fire—the luminescent electrical discharge sometimes observed on masts during storms) and the wind fortuitously died down.

The destination of the Fleet's last expedition is the subject of a recent popular but controversial book by the retired British submarine commander Gavin Menzies: *1421: The Year China Discovered America*. In it, he argues that between 1421 and 1423 different branches of Zheng He's fleet rounded the southern tip of Africa, reached North and South America, circumnavigated the globe, and discovered Australia. Certainly, the discovery of Australia is quite likely, given the extensive Chinese naval presence in Southeast Asia, and it's certainly possible that they could have reached the tip of Africa. If they then rounded the African continent at the Cape of Good Hope, the wind and current pattern of the South Atlantic would have made it very difficult, if not impossible, for them to turn around unless they headed south into the stormy westerly winds of the great Southern Ocean—the roaring forties. It would have been easier for them to continue on a northwesterly route to the Americas.

How far the sixth expedition of the Treasure Fleet actually traveled is a moot point, but it's fun to speculate. There does seem to be evidence of a Chinese presence on the west coast of North America dating back to the Ming period, but an eastbound crossing of the North Pacific from China to America would have been a more likely "downwind" route. But it's worth keeping an open mind on the question—not long ago, only a few enthusiasts believed that the Vikings had ever set eyes on North America!

Arrival

MOONSHINER continued to enjoy perfect weather as we sailed south over a sparkling ocean while Keith spent hours looking expectantly at his fishing lines. In the meantime, Fluke took the whole adventure in her stride, like the old sea dog she obviously was. She was totally devoted to Lot and followed her around continually. If Lot was on deck, then that's where we'd find Fluke, sitting in the cockpit next to her. And when Lot came off watch and went below, then so did Fluke.

Keeping Fluke supplied with fresh food turned out to be easier than we had imagined. One morning we heard the sound of her eating something on deck, and looked up just in time to see her finishing off the remains of a flying fish that had come aboard during the night. It must have made a delicious breakfast treat, because a morning tour of the deck, looking for flying fish, immediately became part of her daily routine.

The next day Keith's persistence with rod and line paid off when he hauled aboard a beautiful dorado. Fluke, of course, claimed her share and was delighted with this further addition to her diet. Then, just before our landfall in the Philippines, Keith hooked a magnificent sailfish. After a considerable fight we brought it alongside and started to haul it over the lifelines. I took one look at the monster—it was well over six feet long, with an enormous and hungry looking mouth—and suggested that maybe it was a wee bit too big for our tiny cockpit. But Keith wasn't keen on giving up his prize. Fortunately the problem was resolved when the fish, having chewed a foot-wide hole in our safety netting, escaped just as we were heaving it aboard.

The weather remained good for the rest of the voyage, and

it grew progressively hotter as we traveled further south. The only problem we experienced was a blow-out of the high-pressure hose on our compressor-driven refrigeration system, and so we ate a lot of frozen food very quickly—before it had time to go bad in the tropical heat. Finally, at dawn, six days after leaving Hong Kong we dropped anchor at our destination.

Zheng He and the Treasure Fleet

Zheng was born into a poor Muslim family in Yunnan Province in southwest China, just north of the border with Laos. He was captured at the age of ten when the army invaded Yunnan and, as was common with boy prisoners, he was castrated at the age of 13. He was then placed in the service of the 25-year-old Prince of Han, Zhu Di, who was destined to become Emperor after usurping the throne of his nephew. Zheng distinguished himself over the next ten years fighting alongside the young prince, first on the frontier and later in his battle for the throne. By the time Zhu Di became Emperor, Zheng He, who was reputed to be an enormous man almost seven feet tall, was a trusted and battle-hardened campaigner. In return for his services to the Emperor he was given command of the Imperial Treasure Fleet.

The Fleet was provisioned to be able to remain at sea for up to three months, and soil was carried aboard to permit the crews to grow fresh food and so avoid the scourge of scurvy that was to plague later European expeditions. They were also able to distill fresh water from seawater. In addition to soldiers, sailors, migrants and traders, the Fleet also carried high-ranking foreign envoys and ambassadors who were entertained while onboard by a bevy of concubines. In his book *1421: The Year China Discovered America*, Gavin Menzies paints an entertaining picture of the life of these women.

They were Tankas, an ethnic group that had migrated from the Chinese interior to the coast and were often engaged in pearl fishing. Their role was not unlike that of the traditional Japanese geisha, and they were similarly trained in the social arts of singing, acting and dancing and could play games such as chess or cards. Their main function was to provide entertainment and sexual services to the foreign officials. In a society where all men were free to take concubines, their profession was not seen as a cause for disgrace, but as a necessary and integral part of society. As Menzies points out, sex was seen as a sanctified act "modeled after heaven." Various sex aids and aphrodisiacs were available to their guests, and amongst the most popular was a pair of red lizards caught while copulating and drowned in a jar of wine. The wine was then left for a year before being consumed. If an envoy wished to keep a favorite concubine she was permitted to leave the vessel with him at his destination. But if no such offer was made, as she grew older she would be given the job of training the younger women. Death was the penalty for any sailor who was found anywhere near their quarters.

7. Puerto Galera Landfall

Puerto Galera is one of those perfect tropical anchorages that fuel the dreams of cruising folk. A totally protected bay surrounded by palm-lined beaches, its name originates from its use by the Spanish, centuries ago, as a secure harbor where they could repair and maintain their galleons—safe from the storms and typhoons that plague the Philippines. But for Lot and me it represented much more than a beautiful destination. The passage from Hong Kong was the final stage in a journey that had taken not six days, but eight years of hard work, planning, and good luck to accomplish. Puerto Galera was the gateway to a new life, and marked the beginning of a voyage that would take MOONSHINER to four continents and across twenty thousand miles of ocean. But that was still in the future, and our first priority on that beautiful morning was to celebrate our safe arrival in paradise; it was time to party.

The previous night had been stressful as we approached our landfall, in pitch-black darkness, through the narrow Verde Island Passage between the islands of Luzon and Mindoro. The Sailing Directions for the Philippines warned that the area was subject to heavy offshore squalls between four and ten o'clock in the morning—the time of our arrival. As we approached our destination we monitored our position carefully with radar and the GPS, but our wind remained fair and the feared squalls failed to materialize. As the coastline emerged from the darkness in the first light of dawn, we were less than five miles from our destination, and we entered the enchanting bay just as the sun was breaking clear of the horizon.

Despite the early hour, we couldn't resist the temptation to announce our arrival by blowing the air-horn as we dropped anchor alongside other regatta boats that had arrived before us. Nautical tradition says that the sun should be above the yardarm before drinks can be served. "It's not even above the trees, let alone the yardarm," observed Lot. "We don't have a yardarm," I explained as I opened the first beer. It soon became obvious that our limited liquor supply wasn't going to sustain the party for very long and it was time to seek new supplies. Lot and Keith somehow managed to assemble the inflatable dinghy while swimming in the bay (they thought it would be fun to try!) and we all headed ashore, where we soon discovered a small bar on the beach.

Fluke Goes Missing

It was soon after arriving in Puerto Galera that we learned that Fluke loved to swim. Early each morning we started the day with a wake-up dip in the bay. No sooner would Lot and I hit the water than Fluke would join us with a mighty splash. She swam fast, with just the tip of her nose, eyes and ears visible. Afterwards, we would take the dinghy ashore and walk into the village, an excursion Fluke loved. She would balance high on the bow of the inflatable, ignoring the flying spray, ears blown back by the wind, eyes wide open, and her mouth working in excitement. As we got close to the shore, unable to contain her enthusiasm, she would leap overboard to swim the final few yards, and then trot happily ahead of us into town. Fluke's swimming prowess soon became well known amongst our cruising friends. One of her "party tricks" was to climb the boarding ladder from the water into the boat—the only help she needed was a gentle hand behind the neck to keep her weight forward.

One morning we loaded the dinghy with containers to

replenish our water supply. As this left no room for Fluke we reluctantly left her on deck, where she stood staring reproachfully after us as we sped away. When we returned an hour later, to our horror, there was no sign of her. Realizing that she must have jumped off the boat in an attempt to follow us, we immediately retraced our route and frantically searched the area, but to no avail. Fluke had disappeared.

The bay at Puerto Galera is over a mile wide, and once she started swimming she was probably too low in the water to see clearly and had become disoriented. In desperation we returned ashore and offered a reward to the village children if they could find her. Soon we had an army of small volunteers scouring the foreshore, while we concentrated on searching the water from the dinghy. We were about a quarter mile from land when Lot suddenly yelled: "Look, I think I see something further out." As we got closer, to our immense relief, we could make out a pair of ears and a nose, just above the surface. I'm not sure who was more relieved as we dragged our exhausted buddy, her tail wagging furiously, into the boat. It had been over two hours since we started looking for her, and over three hours since we first left her behind. It was a mistake we vowed never to make again.

The Wizard and his Friends

We had already lost our refrigeration system en route to Puerto Galera, and shortly after our arrival our new radar also decided to give up the ghost. We'd become reconciled to the idea that they would both be out of action until we reached a larger town with repair facilities, when someone suggested we visit the *wizard*. "If anyone can fix them, he can," we were told. Wizard was the nickname of Mark, an Englishman who had been trained as an electronic technician in the British Army, and had settled in Puerto Galera with his Filipina wife and baby daughter. He made a living repairing boats and fixing electronic equipment, and his nickname bore testimony to his reputation—in no time at all the refrigerator was back in operation.

He also identified the gremlins that plagued the radar set, but we had to wait until we reached Singapore before we could find the parts necessary to get it working again.

Mark was the first of many colorful and enterprising people we would meet on our voyage, whose dreams had led them to an expatriate lifestyle in some of the planet's most beautiful and exotic backwaters. Having escaped into our own brand of freedom, our world was suddenly full of people who, each in their own way, had discovered theirs. Mark's friends Phil and Paul were also good examples.

"Does anyone have any spare air?" asked Phil. "I need to refill my spear-gun." We were chatting with a group of diving friends on the beach. "Help yourself," someone volunteered. We all gathered around, intrigued to see how he was going to fill the compressed air cartridge that powered his underwater spear gun, using a scuba tank. It was easy. He simply connected a high-pressure hose between the two tanks, and bled off the air from the scuba equipment. There was only one problem; diving tanks are filled to a standard pressure of 3,000 pounds per square inch, but marked in bold letters on Phil's aging spear gun was the warning: DO NOT EXCEED 1800 PSI. Undeterred, he happily filled his container to almost twice the recommended pressure limit. The circle of onlookers widened as everyone stepped back from the expected explosion. "No problem there, mate," said Phil in his broad Australian accent. "Just gives her a bit more oomph." This was something of an understatement; later, when we went diving with Phil, we saw his awesome weapon in action—it could have penetrated the hull of a submarine and probably come out the other side.

Phil had retired after a career as deep-sea diver for a large marine company. He'd married a local girl, and settled down with her in Puerto Galera to raise their three children and work on whatever local dive jobs he could find.

Without doubt the most beautiful yacht in the anchorage was SONIC. She was a 60-foot steel beauty that had been almost completely rebuilt by Paul, her American owner. After serving as a helicopter pilot in Vietnam at the age of 20, an experience he considered himself lucky to have survived, he moved to the Philippines where he discovered SONIC in an advanced stage of decay, and decided to restore her. He began by replacing almost 40% of the steel hull plating—a mammoth job on such a large boat, given the lack of equipment at his disposal. With gung-ho enthusiasm and ingenuity he rigged a block and tackle, and used a system of jacks to slowly bend the heavy replacement panels into shape. After countless hours of work, the final result was a steel boat with a rounded hull as smooth and fair as the day she first left the shipyard.

He tested her seaworthiness on three subsequent return crossings of the Pacific from the Philippines to California, and on his last trip he was pounded for three days in storm-force winds off the Aleutian Islands. Although the boat sustained major damage to her deck gear, some of which was still visible, she had suffered no major structural problems. But he swore that on any future trips he would make a point of keeping south of latitude 40° North. Paul was in the process of building and installing cement mooring buoys in the bay, so that more boats could fit into the small anchorage without damaging the coral. Like Mark and Phil, Paul had made the Philippines his home, and he and his partner were expecting their first baby at any moment. All three friends were living their dream, using their ingenuity and skills to make a living.

8. A Close Call

It all started one evening in Hong Kong, when we were planning our vacation for the following summer. "Why don't we learn to dive?" suggested Lot. "I've always wanted to try, and it would be useful when we go sailing." It made sense, and after doing some research we signed up for lessons with a diving school in Kuala Lumpur a few months later. After completing the basic training in a city swimming pool, we finished the course with a series of ocean dives in the Perhentian Islands. These ocean jewels, which are located off Malaysia's northeast coast close to the border with Thailand, offer some of the best diving in the world. We were thrilled by the sight of unspoiled coral, brilliantly colored nudibranches, giant clams, and an endless variety of fish, including enormous bump-head wrasse. The following year we decided to take another diving holiday, this time on the Philippine Island of Negros Oriental.

"We don't have much experience," we warned Boyette, our Filipino guide for the week. "We've only made six dives in the open ocean." "No problem, the diving's easy around here," he laughed. We liked Boyette; he was friendly, outgoing, and good company. Born in the local village, he had started out in life as a reef fisherman, free-diving the local coral in search of fish with only a snorkel, makeshift mask, and an old spear gun. But Boyette had a dream too—that one day he would run his own business. Somehow he had saved the money to build a small beach café. It had done well, and eventually he was able to expand it into a fully-fledged bar and restaurant. Finally, he added more space and opened an adjoining diving school and guide service, which was quickly becoming popular.

On our first evening with Boyette we were entertained by the antics of the "Pissed Pig," as his family's resident porker was aptly named. The animal lived behind the house, and every day he was fed a regular diet of beer slops left over from the bar to fatten him up. When he wasn't drunk, or sleeping off the effects of his most recent binge, his favorite pastime was being taken for a walk on the beach on his leash, followed by an invigorating swim in the sea. He'd become a family pet, and I don't know if he eventually escaped the cooking pot, but he was leading a heck of a life in the meantime.

Next morning we crossed the narrow Tanon Strait to the southern tip of the island of Cebu. We planned to make two dives—one in the late morning and another in the early afternoon after a short rest. Our first dive was in 30 feet of clear water, and the reef, as Boyette had promised, looked beautiful in the filtered sunlight. We had been on the bottom for perhaps 15 minutes when the current began to pick up speed. It increased rapidly, and soon we were being swept along by an underwater "river" at four or five knots. In our inexperience we were oblivious to the dangerous situation that was developing, and we enjoyed the spectacular sleigh ride; coral heads materialized eerily out the blue void and appeared to accelerate as they glided silently past before retreating into the gloom. I looked up and was reassured to see that the surface was clearly visible. Suddenly Boyette, who only moments before had been just ahead of us, was nowhere in sight. Then I saw him again; the reef had come to an abrupt end at an enormous underwater cliff that disappeared into the blue-black depths below. Boyette had ducked down just below the edge of the chasm and gestured for us to join him. We had arrived at the end of the island.

We lay on the lip of the underwater precipice, holding onto pieces of coral just beneath the main force of the current. The coral garden through which we had been carried seemed so close, and yet the speed of the particles of sand and organic material rushing past just above our heads made it clear it was impossible to swim back in that direction. I raised my arm and it was immediately knocked backwards by the force of the water. But I still assumed that this must all be part of a normal day's diving in this part of the world.

We looked towards Boyette for an indication of what we should do next, and he gestured that we should let go of our tenuous hold on the coral. We nodded our agreement, and as soon as he released his grip we did the same. I had no sensation of movement as the reef and precipice accelerated smoothly away from me before disappearing into the blue universe in which we now hung suspended; it was like watching a video of the receding Earth, taken from a rocket as it is launched into orbit. The current must have been incredibly smooth because there was no turbulence: our new world was silent, calm, and surreal. We were only a few feet apart, and our proximity seemed to offer security as we hung together like slow motion dancers caught in a spotlight through the blue translucence. Boyette gestured, "Are you OK?" "Yes," we signaled in reply. We started kicking slowly towards the surface, making sure that we followed the textbook procedure of rising no faster than the smallest bubbles we exhaled; there was something immensely reassuring about those three columns of air as they rose towards the surface and safety. Everything seemed normal.

Time passed, and I began to feel a strange disquiet—not alarm, but a sense of unease that I couldn't quite put my finger on. I looked around. Everything seemed normal; we were all kicking slowly towards the surface, and our bubbles were rising at what looked like the correct speed for a normal rate of ascent. What was it? There was something wrong. But what? Suddenly, I realized that it was getting darker. I looked up towards the surface, but it was no longer visible. I looked down at my depth gauge, and decided that it must be reading incorrectly because it said we were at a depth of 120 feet—almost 100 feet deeper than when we let go of the reef. I wasn't afraid, only puzzled that somehow my brain wasn't interpreting the information correctly. I remember tapping the depth gauge, irrationally thinking that something must have stuck, although how it could have stuck at a level 100 feet below its previous reading, and simultaneously made the surface disappear, were insights that only occurred to me later. I looked across at Lot and Boyette, but if they knew something was wrong they gave no sign of it. But the tropical current, warm and seductive, was carrying us inexorably deeper into the sea.

Suddenly Boyette gave an unmistakable gesture that we must head for the surface in earnest. We inflated our buoyancy jackets and started kicking vigorously. We began to rise through the thousand of bubbles that we had exhaled in the preceding minutes; it was like swimming up through an enormous glass of champagne, with bubbles surging and sparkling around us as the water slowly brightened. Finally, we broke surface and Boyette, out of either sheer relief or adrenaline induced exuberance, kept shouting "Special whirlpool dive . . . special whirlpool dive by Boyette." The surface of the ocean was alive with moving slicks of oil-smooth water, alternating with areas of choppy waves, clear evidence that an invisible river was in full flood below. Fortunately, our chartered dive boat had been following the track of our bubbles, and was able to pick us up almost immediately.

On reflection it was apparent what had happened. The strong current, as it flows off the end of the island shelf into the depths below, begins to oscillate up and down over a vertical range of hundreds of meters. It's like the effect that produces wave cloud when a strong and steady wind blows over a mountain range. We had been caught in the down portion of the oscillation, and the smaller bubbles we were exhaling were only rising relative to ourselves; we, and they, were being carried ever deeper by the powerful flow of water. I don't know if Boyette had experienced the phenomenon before; I suspect not, but he wasn't about to admit that he'd got us into a situation beyond his control. Fortune often favors the foolish, and we got away with a situation that could have become fatal if we'd panicked. But panic requires perception of a danger, and our ignorance kept us calm.

Later the same week we saw the evidence of extensive reef damage in the area. Boyette said that dynamite fishing carried out by the local villagers caused most of the destruction. I suppose they were caught in a vicious cycle: as the availability of fish declined they resorted to ever more destructive techniques to catch the quantity necessary for survival. Boyette was doing his best to educate the people with the idea that preserving the reefs was in their own best interest. And with this objective in mind he asked if we would mind taking along one of his old spearfishing chums on a dive to a reef that was within a "marine protected area." He wanted him to see for himself how much more plentiful the fish were when blasting hadn't damaged the reef.

Getting to the dive site was an adventure in itself, as it was located on a small inaccessible island a considerable distance from Boyette's base. We drove first to the fishing village where Boyette had made arrangements to pick up a boat. "Is there any reason you chose this particular village?" I asked on the way. "Yes," he said. "The crossing to the island is often rough and these guys are the best seamen on the coast—they have to be, because they control the smuggling trade between here and Mindanao." We made the three-mile crossing to the dive site in a small open boat with a single outrigger float. Before we left, the headman in the village chose a skipper from the crowd of young men standing around. I was glad that Boyette seemed to know the villagers well, because our selected captain looked like a cross between Al Capone and the triad villain in a Kung Fu movie. He wore an American style army helmet, camouflage battle dress, and a permanent scowl that signaled: keep your distance. Frankly, I wouldn't have wanted to meet him in an alley after dark, but perhaps I'm being uncharitable and he was a nice guy having an off day.

Boyette's boyhood diving friend had been quiet during the journey. He was a small powerfully built man, who dove with only minimal equipment: an old snorkel and homemade goggles were his only gear. "How far down does he work?" we asked Boyette. "About a hundred and twenty feet," was the astounding reply. Frankly, we were skeptical that anyone could dive this deep without carrying air, let alone fish. But later, when we were admiring some coral on the reef wall at around 60 feet, he suddenly passed us and disappeared into the depths below. It was several minutes before he reappeared, and passed us again on his way back to the surface. At the end of the dive Boyette was furious to discover that his old friend had abused the rules of the reserve by catching and killing a mid-sized octopus. Old habits obviously die hard, and ecology is a hard sell to someone with an empty belly.

9. Heading South

After five glorious weeks in Puerto Galera it was time to move on. Keith and Vanessa had already left, so MOONSHINER's crew consisted of myself as skipper, Lot as first mate, and of course Fluke—who was in charge of security and morale. We planned to spend a few days on the island of Palawan, where friends from the Aberdeen Marina had bought land and were developing a small farm. We hadn't seen them for six months, and we were anxious to find out how their venture was progressing.

On the eve of our departure Fred rowed out to MOONSHINER with his wife to say goodbye. Fred, or Baron Frederick van Pallandt to use his correct title, was a Dutch aristocrat who thirty years earlier had achieved fame, with his first wife Nina, in the singing and guitar playing duo, *Nina and Frederick*. For a long time they had their own successful weekly program on BBC television in the UK. Fred was now living in Puerto Galera, and his sailboat was anchored in the harbour close to MOONSHINER.

He told us the story of how he met his wife—a girl from one of the South Pacific Islands he had visited during his circumnavigation many years earlier. During his stay they fell in love, but she wasn't sure she wanted to leave her island home and follow his gypsy lifestyle. She arrived at the marina on the day of his departure, clutching a small suitcase containing all her possessions. But she couldn't bring herself to make the final break and step aboard; she stood on the dock in an anguish of indecision. "I'm leaving now," said Fred. "Are you coming or not? It is up to you." She thought hard. "Only if you promise to stop smoking," she said. "OK, it's a deal," he replied.

After asking us about our plans, Fred looked thoughtful for a moment and then said, "MOONSHINER is very small for such a long journey. You'll find it a lot less intimidating if you think about it in stages, and only worry about one stage at a time." We thanked him for his advice, which has been part of our sailing philosophy ever since, and happily accepted the bottle of excellent wine he offered as a going away present. Sadly, we were never to see either of them again. Some years later, after we arrived in Europe, we were stunned to learn that soon after our departure they had both been murdered, apparently by thugs who broke into their house in the middle of the night. As far as I know, no suspects were ever arrested.

The next morning, just as we were leaving, Paul from SONIC rowed over and asked, "Are you going anywhere near Boayan Island?" "Yes. Well, fairly close anyway, we'll pass it after we've visited Palawan," we said. "I have some photographs for an old friend of mine, Apolinario, who lives on Boayan. Everyone there knows him. Would you be willing to drop them off?" We said we'd be delighted, and moments later we raised our anchor and once again pointed MOONSHINER's bow towards the horizon.

At dawn, two days later, we were five miles northwest of Palawan, near the village of El Nido where we planned to anchor for the night. The area was dotted with spectacular and fantastically shaped islets with multi-colored vertical cliffs and needle sharp peaks. They took on the outline of wild animals: here was a hippo molded in stone, and over there lurked a colorful rocky wild boar. The scenery was spectacular, but our Philippine Sailing Guide warned that the inhabitants of some of the islands were hostile to visitors, and one was notorious for posting armed guards as lookouts to dissuade the curious. Guns are easy to obtain in many parts of the Philippines; we could buy a local copy of an AK47 automatic rifle for as little as $15. The islands, we decided, were best admired from a distance.

"I don't like the look of this," I said to Lot as we approached the anchorage. "I think we almost hit that one." We were still inexperienced in the art of judging the depth of coral heads, which rose like brown mushrooms above the sandy seabed, and we became more apprehensive as we got closer to land, and they increased in frequency. This last near miss brought us to a halt while we decided whether to continue. "Let's go somewhere else," was Lot's opinion. "We're still a long way from shore, and the depth sounder says we're already in less than four meters of water. And I think the coral's getting closer to the surface." As MOONSHINER draws two meters we certainly didn't have much water to spare under the keel, and so we agreed to continue on our way and look for a less stressful spot to spend the night.

As it was too late to reach our destination in Malampaya Sound before dark we consulted the chart for an alternative anchorage, and decided to make for a protected inlet a few miles ahead known as Port Kataaba. It was now the middle of May, and the *Sailing Directions* for the Philippines warn that thunderstorms are common on Palawan's west coast between May and October. As we approached the narrow entrance to the protected bay the sky began to darken. Suddenly, we were hit by a wall of rain and wind—lightning flashed around us, and the nearby cliffs reverberated with the crash of thunder. The squall struck with amazing speed, and reduced visibility almost to zero; the shoreline, only a few hundred meters away, was completely obscured as horizontal sheets of water hissed by the cockpit, and the sea and the sky merged into a single furious element. But in less than 15 minutes it started to clear, and the phenomenon was over as quickly as it had begun. We entered the bay a few minutes later, shaking water from our hair, and spent a quiet night at anchor without a breath of wind or a drop of rain to disturb our sleep.

The next morning, under a clear and windless sky, we powered through narrow Endeavour Strait with a strong following current, which rushed us passed the wooden houses of the village of Liminangcong lining the shore. We kept a close watch on the depth sounder to avoid the many areas of shallow water in the narrow passage, and soon emerged into the tranquil water of Malampaya Sound. The sound cuts 20 miles into the undeveloped and sparsely populated rainforest of northwest Palawan, to form one of the best natural harbors in the Philippines. Two hours later we were relaxing at anchor, in front of our friend's house.

Mount Capoas

Malampaya Sound is bordered to the west by the Capoan Peninsula—named after Mount Capoas, which at just over 3,300 feet dominated the skyline near our anchorage. One afternoon, towards the end of our visit, we were relaxing on our friend's balcony admiring the mountain in the late afternoon sun when I asked: "How easy is it to climb to the top? Do you know anyone who's done it?" "There's no trail," he replied. "A couple of German guys hiked up it last year with a guide. It's not rock climbing—the biggest problem is getting through the jungle growth and avoiding the mosquitoes and wild pigs." As an afterthought, he added: "Why, are you looking for some exercise?" "Sure," I said with a bravado induced by his endless supply of rum. "Where do I find the guide?" I looked towards Lot. "Forget it," she said. "You're on your own if you want to go marauding through the jungle. Count me out—I'll stay here and relax." Well why not, I thought, it's not everyday you get the chance to conquer a tropical mountain.

The arrangements were made the next day, and the following morning I was met at the beach by my guide, Rey, and his young helper. They were both short and wiry, and said little as we climbed into the *banca* to cross the narrow channel that separated our anchorage from the narrow coastal plain in front of the mountain. We stopped briefly at their village—a small cluster of thatched houses in a clearing in the tropical rain forest—while they collected supplies of food and water. Rey's house was built on stilts, and children laughed and played on matting scattered on the floor, while chickens ran free on the dry earth beneath the buildings. The older villagers stared and smiled, presumably happy to tolerate another crazy foreigner willing to pay for the privilege of climbing a mountain for no useful purpose.

At first the going was flat and easy, with a clearly marked trail leading through a forest of large trees. But the path soon began to climb. It became increasingly steep, and harder to follow as the undergrowth thickened around us. Soon, we were hacking our way upward through a tangle of clawing branches using our machetes, as the larger trees near the coast gave way to dense low lying bush. The vegetation grew thicker the higher we climbed, and it was slow and exhausting work on the steep slope. As the sun climbed in the sky the day grew hotter, and our rest stops became more frequent. "Where did you learn to use a machete?" I asked Rey, during a break while we ate some lunch. "In Mindanao," he replied. "I was there for two years. In the army, fighting the rebels."

I didn't envy him the experience. The fiercely independent Muslim inhabitants of the southern Philippines, the Moros, have fought against outside intervention since the Spanish first arrived in the sixteenth century. Over the last 30 years thousands of military and civilian lives have been lost in the ongoing conflict on Mindanao, as the Moros fought to establish an independent Muslim state. Hundreds of thousands more have fled the area as refugees, and we later met some of these people after MOONSHINER arrived in Sabah, East Malaysia. A particularly ruthless and militant branch of the independence movement, Abu Sayyaf, has recently gained international notoriety for the brutal kidnapping and murder of foreigners. Against this background I viewed Rey's jungle skills with new respect.

We had taken supplies for a two-day trip. Our objective was to get as far as possible the first day and then spend the night on the mountain before heading for the summit early in the morning, before the day became too hot. Rey had insisted that it wasn't necessary to take sleeping bags, and I had taken his advice. If I'd realized at the time that his idea of acceptable comfort was nurtured in the jungles of Mindanao fighting rebels, I wouldn't have been so quick to agree. We continued slowly up the hill through the afternoon heat and finally, at around four, we called a halt and began to prepare our camp for the night.

We found a fairly smooth piece of ground beneath a small overhanging cliff, where the vegetation wasn't too thick. After clearing away the underbrush, Rey and his friend took a long length of rope, tied pieces of foliage and branches to it, and then strung it up in the trees around our makeshift home for the night. "What's that for?" I asked, puzzled. "In case wild pigs come close. We can hear them when they hit the rope," Rey replied. "Are they dangerous?" I asked. They looked at each other and smiled; my question obviously didn't warrant a reply. We slept that night on branches that we laid on the hard dry ground, and I can't speak for my companions, but I was far too tired to worry about the possible threat. But the night was quiet and uneventful, and we got underway again just after dawn.

We reached the summit after two more hours of hard climbing. It took a while before we could find a gap in the vegetation big enough to see through, but once we did the view was superb. To the west, in the distance and 3,000 feet below us, the silver-blue water of Palawan Strait sparkled through gaps in the cotton wool clouds. All the effort suddenly seemed worthwhile, and even my companions thought that reaching the top was an achievement worth savoring for a while. Eventually, we reluctantly started back down the mountain, following our old trail amongst the rocks and clinging underbrush. We were about two thirds of the way to the village, and had reached flatter land, when we heard sounds ahead of us in the forest.

"Stay here and don't move until we come back," said Rey. My guides went ahead, and rapidly disappeared from sight amongst the trees. I waited, wondering what was happening, and was relieved when they reappeared a few minutes later and beckoned me to follow. We continued down the trail, and after a few hundred meters came to a group of men leading oxen that were dragging logs out of the forest. They stared sullenly as we passed and said nothing. Later, Rey explained that they were running an illegal logging operation, and they didn't want strangers seeing their activities. "I explained that you weren't a problem," he said, whatever that meant. When we finally reached the beach the small *banca* we had left behind the day before had disappeared; we were fortunate that after waiting for an hour, we were able to hail another boat as it passed close to shore and hitch a ride across the inlet. Our climb of Mount Capoas may never be recorded in the annals of mountaineering history, but it was an experience I wouldn't have missed— although Lot still thinks I was crazy.

A Message from the Ocean

We had spent almost a week with our friends, and once again it was time to move on. So the next day we said goodbye to Malampaya Sound, and watched Mount Capoas disappear into the distance as we motored out of the anchorage towards our rendezvous with Paul's friend, Apolinario, on Boayan Island.

We arrived at our destination six hours later and dropped anchor, late in the afternoon, in a gorgeous bay about a quarter-mile from the shore. The island was stunningly beautiful; the sun slowly slipped into the sea under a red and mauve sky as the palm trees stood in dark profile against the sunset. The only sounds were from the wind and the low breaking surf on the beach.

Lot decided to swim to shore, accompanied by Fluke, with the letter and photographs secured in a watertight bag. As the two of them waded through the surf, the daylight almost gone, she saw an elderly woman watching from the edge of the beach. "Do you know Apollinario? We have a package for him," asked Lot. The woman's jaw fell as she stared at this apparition—a dog and a lycra-suited blonde appearing from out of the ocean. MOONSHINER lay behind a curve in the otherwise deserted bay, and wasn't visible in the dying light—there was no logical place from which they could have come. "Yes, but he lives at the other end of the island," she said at last. As it was already late and getting dark, she offered to make sure that the letter and photographs were delivered the next day. Lot thanked her, and together with Fluke, disappeared back into the ocean as the woman stared after them. As a method of mail delivery I'm sure it remains unique.

Tropical Storms

Boayan Island was our last stop in the Philippines. Our next destination was Sabah—part of the Federation of Malaysia on the island of Borneo, 300 miles to the southwest. We sailed at first under a "good weather" tropical sky—bright blue and dotted with the small, friendly, cotton wool balls of white cumulus clouds. But soon after midday the cumulus to the east, over Palawan Island, began growing ominously, and by late afternoon they had developed into towering thunderheads—massive castles in the sky that began to drift offshore directly into our path. In the tropics the sun sinks steeply towards the horizon, and night falls quickly. As the daylight faded we heard rumblings of thunder, and saw lightning ahead. We started counting the seconds between the flashes and the explosions that followed, trying to calculate how far away it was. The period got shorter and shorter until the storm finally enveloped us.

The last traces of daylight disappeared. We were afloat in a black void that was illuminated every few seconds by blinding flashes of lightning that seared the retina; the world around us was shattered with a crescendo of thunderclaps that left the mind numb. The storm off El Nido had been bad, but it was nothing compared to this. Again and again the lightning struck the nearby water. Two jagged tracers of light cut through the night, and simultaneously hit the sea on opposite sides of the boat. The instantaneous explosion felt as if MOONSHINER had been blown apart. We were completely helpless in the face of the onslaught and a terrified Fluke had long ago disappeared into the cabin. In a gale you can take action to protect yourself, but in a tropical thunderstorm you're a helpless spectator.

Between the reverberations of thunder we had to shout to each other to make ourselves heard over the roar of the torrential rain, as it beat furiously on the cabin roof and pounded the seas around us flat.

I looked up at our aluminum mast. It was mounted on a steel deck on a steel boat that was floating in a salt-water conductor in the worst electrical storm I had ever experienced, or even imagined. And if that wasn't enough, it was also the tallest object within a 40-mile radius—it was hard to imagine a more perfect lightning conductor. I was convinced that it wasn't a question of *if* we would be hit, but *when*. Throughout the storm the wind remained moderate, but as a precaution we'd furled the foresail and put a double reef in the main when we saw the thunderheads approaching. We'd also turned off most of our electrical equipment, and disconnected as much of it as possible. There was nothing else we could do except to try to keep clear of the metal fittings, which in a steel boat is quite a challenge, admire the frightening beauty of the spectacle, and hope that somehow we wouldn't be hit. We stayed off the deck and kept watch from the companionway, while the boat steered herself on the autopilot. We considered turning that off too, but I didn't relish standing in the soaking cockpit, hanging on to a steel wheel.

For some reason, at the height of the storm, I remembered an anecdote about why cows are more likely than people to be killed by lightning. I didn't remember the details, but it had to do with the idea that the voltage in the ground was at a maximum at the point where the lightning struck, and it dissipated the further away you were from that point. Since current is caused by the voltage differential, the author argued that the further apart your legs were, the greater the jolt would be. Hence cows were more vulnerable. At the time I thought the idea was amusing, but I didn't believe a word of it. I still didn't, but I put my feet closer together anyway.

The lightning began to abate at around two o'clock in the morning, and we were amazed to have survived the storm unscathed. But the following night was a repeat of the first. We watched apprehensively as the thunderheads thickened and rolled off the coastal mountains, and then drifted out to sea in the late afternoon. From dusk until the early hours of the morning we were subjected to another onslaught by a violent electrical storm, accompanied by torrential rain, but very little wind. Again, MOONSHINER must have benefited from an unseen guardian, for although it seemed that we could reach out and touch the lightning that was exploding all around us, we never suffered a strike and none of our electrical equipment was damaged.

We were lucky to have escaped. We've met several sailors who have suffered direct strikes which "fried" all their electronic equipment. One friend, on seeing a squall approach, wrapped up his hand-held GPS in an old sock and put it in a clothing drawer, well away from any wiring. But it was still destroyed, along with all his other electrical gear, when the boat was hit. Another sailor we know had his electronics wiped out by the powerful magnetic field of a near miss—without the lightning actually hitting his boat. Fortunately, in all the cases we've heard about, there's been relatively little damage to the boats themselves.

If for no other reason than the danger of electrical storms, it's essential for offshore sailors to carry a sextant, even in this age of electronics, and know how to use it. I once asked a skipper what kind of sextant he carried onboard, and he replied that he didn't need one. "I use GPS," he explained. "But what if you get hit by lightning?" I asked. He gave me a self-satisfied smile. "I've got three. One mounted in the boat and two hand-helds." Now backup equipment is a great idea if you can afford it, as insurance against mechanical failure. But the only way backups offer insurance against lightning strikes is if the equipment is mounted on different boats. I wished him well.

Typhoon Waters

Although the thunderstorms we experienced off the west coast of Palawan were unpleasant, they were nothing compared with what Mother Nature sometimes inflicts on the region. As we got closer to Sabah we were relieved that we were finally leaving an area threatened by nature's most devastating phenomenon—the tropical cyclone. In the western North Pacific these storms are called typhoons. Sabah has long been known to seafarers as "The land below the wind," meaning that it lies safely to the south of the typhoon belt. The area through which we'd been traveling since leaving Hong Kong experiences more of these storms than anywhere else on earth, and they are also the largest and most intense. The region averages over 25 tropical storms each year, of which 18 can be expected to develop into full-blown typhoons. This compares with an average of 9 tropical storms in the North Atlantic and Caribbean, of which 5 become hurricanes in a typical year.

A tropical storm becomes a typhoon when its sustained wind speed reaches 64 knots (74 mph). The designation "Super Typhoon" is applied when sustained winds exceed 130 knots (150 mph). But this figure fails to communicate the awesome power of these vast whirlpools of violence. One way to put them in perspective is to consider that many fully developed typhoons, over the open ocean, achieve sustained winds of 140 to 150 knots sometime during their life cycle. Extreme gusts frequently exceed the maximum sustained wind by 30% to 50%—so a 150-knot typhoon can have gusts of 225 knots (260 mph). The amount of energy this represents is hard to comprehend. After World War II, meteorologists became fond of expressing a typhoon's power in terms of the explosive impact of atomic bombs. A typical tropical thunderstorm has the energy equivalent of about thirteen 20-kiloton atomic bombs. In a 24-hour period, even a small-scale typhoon will release about 20 billion tons of water, and has an energy equivalent close to 500,000 atomic bombs, or almost six atomic bombs per second.

By our third night at sea we were south of Palawan, and had reached the western edge of Balabac Strait, which separates the Philippine archipelago from the island of Borneo to the south. As there was no nearby land to generate thunderstorms we enjoyed a peaceful night for a change, and the next day dawned without a breath of wind. We motorsailed all morning over a flat blue mirror of a sea and under a cloudless sky. Lot thought she saw a whale in the distance, but it disappeared before we could be certain. At five in the afternoon we anchored in Police Bay, Gaya Island—our landfall in Sabah.

Typhoons in the Philippines and China Sea

On the morning of December 18, 1944, a task force of the US Third Fleet consisting of 13 carriers, 15 cruisers, and about 50 destroyers under the command of Admiral Halsey, was overtaken by Typhoon Cobra with devastating results. They were located 300 miles east of the Philippine island of Luzon, and had just completed three days of raids against Japanese airfields in support of American operations on Mindoro. Many of the ships had attempted to fuel a day earlier, but increasingly rough weather had made it impossible. The exact track and strength of the storm weren't known, but a new rendezvous was chosen that was expected to be clear of its center. Unfortunately, the typhoon took a more southerly course than expected, and by noon on the 18th some of the fleet found itself directly in its path.

Cobra was a relatively small typhoon, but its impact was deadly. Three destroyers, the HULL, SPENCE, and MONAGHAN capsized and sank with the loss of almost all hands.

Two other ships, the DEWEY and the AYLWIN, barely escaped the same fate and six or seven ships were seriously damaged. Fires broke out in three carriers when planes broke loose, and 146 aircraft were destroyed or damaged beyond repair, either by fire, impact, or by being swept overboard. Solid water was scooped up by the decks of even the largest carriers, almost 60 feet above the sea, and the smaller destroyers that were caught in the worst of the storm were unable to change course, and were forced to lie broadside to the wind, rolling to leeward by as much as 70 degrees. Their rudders were useless in the ferocious conditions: at the height of the storm, around noon on the 18th, the mountainous seas were estimated at 70 feet from trough to crest, and the wind was gusting to 120 knots (140 mph). A total of 790 officers and men were killed, and another 80 were injured. The vessels that sank had been particularly vulnerable as their fuel tanks weren't full and they lacked ballast.

Admiral Halsey, who was on the battleship NEW JERSEY, described the typhoon in his autobiography: "No one who has not been through a typhoon can conceive its fury. The seventy-foot seas smash you from all sides. The rain and scud are blinding; they drive you flat out, until you can't tell the ocean from the air. At broad noon I couldn't see the bow of my ship, three-hundred and fifty feet from the bridge . . . this typhoon tossed our enormous ship as if she were a canoe."

Even the largest modern boats are threatened by a typhoon's devastating power. On September 9, 1980, the bulk carrier DERBYSHIRE was en route to Kawasaki, Japan, with a cargo of 165,000 tons of iron ore pellets. She gave her position as 230 miles east of Okinawa. Six hours later, at 0930, she reported that she was hove-to in a violent storm and advised that she would be arriving late at her destination. She was never heard from again, and disappeared without trace and the loss of 44 lives: 42 crew members and 2 officers' wives.

She was built in 1976 by Swan Hunter Shipyards in the UK, and at just under 92,000 gross tons at her launching she was the largest ship of her kind built by the yard. With a length of 965 feet, and a beam of 145 feet, she was enormous: as long as three football fields and wider than a six-lane highway, but her size didn't save her. A 1998 investigation concluded that she was a victim of Typhoon Orchid, and that the hatch covers over her holds had been blown off and the ship had been sunk by the thousands of tons of water that immediately poured into the hull—too quickly for even an SOS to be sent. But family members believe that there was a flaw in the vessel that caused the hull to split under the enormous stresses imposed by the wind and seas. Between 1980 and 1994, 149 bulk and combination carriers were lost at sea, at a cost of 1,144 lives.

10. The Land below the Wind

The evening we arrived at Gaya, Lot decided to go for a quick swim to the beach before dinner. We were a couple of hundred yards from shore, and she'd only gone about a third of the way, when she turned around and tore back towards MOONSHINER, her arms and legs churning the water as if half the sharks in the Pacific were on her heels. "What's the matter? Are you OK?" I shouted as she got close to the boat. She didn't answer until she was back on deck, breathless and looking shaken. "I just got this crazy feeling that there was something near me in the water," she said. "It's so full of algae I couldn't see a thing, but it suddenly freaked me out." She shuddered. Lot's a strong swimmer, and this was out of character—freaking out is something she just doesn't do. But she couldn't explain her sudden fear, and neither of us ventured back into the water during our stay in the bay.

The next day we powered the short distance to the main anchorage for visiting yachts in front of the Tanjung Aru Beach Hotel in the nearby capital, Kota Kinabalu. The protected anchorage is reached by following a narrow buoyed channel that cuts through fringing reefs. But the channel markers were small and hard to see from a distance, so we called the marina on the VHF and they safely guided us in.

Soon after our arrival we were delighted to discover that Graeme, on NEFERTITI, was anchored nearby. Graeme had been our neighbor in Aberdeen Harbour and he had witnessed Fluke's encounter with the marine police. We knew he had been

planning to head south, and we'd been hoping to run into him
again. "You must meet Michel and Frances," he told us soon
after our arrival. "They're Canadians, and I think one of them
even comes from Vancouver. I'm going over to their boat this
afternoon, why don't you come along?" We were about to meet
a couple who have since become close friends, and whose sailing company we have since enjoyed in Asia, Europe, and North
America.

Frances and Michel's story is a great example of how to
bring dreams to life on a small budget. After working for several years with a Canadian NGO in Central America, Michel
found a job as crew with a sailboat delivery skipper. After a
couple of years he had thousands of sea-miles under his belt, including two crossings of the Indian Ocean from Asia to South
Africa, and had saved enough money to look for a small offshore boat of his own. In Perth, Western Australia, he and
Frances discovered a small but seaworthy 30-foot sloop that fit-
ted their budget. They bought her and renamed her PAX. Their
first voyage was a 1,500-mile passage in the infamous Southern
Ocean, from Perth to Sydney. "How did you enjoy the roaring
forties?" I asked them one day. "As soon as we left we decided
we must be crazy," said Michel. "The seas were enormous, but
it was easier to keep going than turn around. We made it to
Sydney in about a week." I looked at Frances to see her reaction; she rolled her eyes and shook her head at the memory.
After leaving Sydney they sailed north to Japan, where they
worked for three years teaching English to build up their cruising funds before setting sail once again, this time bound for
Europe.

For the next two years MOONSHINER and PAX followed
similar routes through Asia, up the Red Sea, and across the
Mediterranean, and we often enjoyed sailing in company. We
parted in Greece, as PAX planned to winter in the Mediterranean
before heading across the Atlantic to Brazil and Argentina, and
we needed to reach Holland to find work and get our own finances back in order. But we stayed in touch. Today, we both
live aboard our boats on Canada's west coast and are almost

neighbors. Their marina is only 30 miles from Vancouver, and we see them regularly.

One of our biggest and most pleasant cruising surprises was to discover how easy it was to make friends. The world's weather patterns require that long distance sailors must follow similar routes, and travel at more or less the same time of year. So we kept bumping into the same people. By the time we reached the Mediterranean, it was a rare anchorage where we didn't recognize at least one familiar boat. Before leaving Hong Kong, we expected that isolation would be the price we must pay for our cruising freedom. We couldn't have been more wrong; we made more friends during our four years of cruising than during any other period in our lives. And we didn't spend all our time underway, either. On average, for each day at sea, we enjoyed seven days at anchor—either socializing or exploring ashore.

The wealth of sailing experience to be found amongst the offshore cruising fleet is amazing. One day, two new boats arrived in our Kota Kinabalu anchorage, each with a middle-aged couple as crew, and Lot rowed over to say hello and invite them over for a sundowner. We were feeling pretty pleased with ourselves at the time, imagining that the 1,000 miles we'd sailed since leaving Hong Kong qualified us as old salts. "How long have you been sailing?" I asked, as they sat relaxing in MOON-SHINER's cockpit. "You don't really want to know," they said, laughing. "We've been cruising together for about 25 years, and we're both in the middle of our third circumnavigation." I was suitably humbled.

Their experience turned out to be valuable to us in an unexpected way. Before leaving Hong Kong, Lot had written to the embassies of the countries we intended to visit to find out what kind of reception Fluke could expect. In reply, we'd accumulated a depressing stack of rules and regulations that promised a real hassle if we followed official procedures. In the Philippines nobody had seemed to care who or what was onboard, just as long as we paid the fees. But in Sabah we had suffered a bureaucratic ritual after we declared the dog, and the health authorities insisted on sending a veterinarian out to MOONSHINER to check Fluke out. The situation wasn't made any easier by the fact that the lady vet who arrived at the anchorage was afraid of the water.

One of the couples had sailed with a dog for many years, and when we told them this story they advised us to stop following official procedure. "Don't try and hide Fluke, but don't make an issue of her either," they advised. We took their advice to heart, and it worked; Fluke's presence on board has never been challenged by any customs or health official in the twenty-eight countries MOONSHINER has visited since leaving Sabah. We kept her vaccination certificates handy in case they were needed, but no official has ever asked to see them. With the exception of Singapore, we have avoided the few countries that would require that Fluke be quarantined during our stay.

Sarawak

After five weeks in Sabah we finally said goodbye to our friends in the anchorage, and set sail down the coast of Borneo towards Sarawak. With a following wind and favorable current we arrived just before nightfall at the island of Labuan, 65 miles to the southwest and anchored in Victoria Harbor, next to an ugly cement factory. It was hardly an idyllic setting, but the town was a free port and a good place to re-provision. During the nineteenth century northern Borneo was home to predatory Malay and Dayak pirates, who attacked vessels traveling between Singapore and Hong Kong. Because of its strategic location at the mouth of Brunei Bay, the Sultan of Brunei ceded Labuan to the British to use as a base from which they could protect shipping in the area. It subsequently became a British colony, and eventually joined Malaysia, along with Sabah and Sarawak, in the 1960s.

We left Victoria the following afternoon, and two days later arrived at Port Bintulu, a large commercial harbor in northern

Sarawak that exports liquefied natural gas. The port has a good reputation amongst yachties—partly because the lagoon, which is used as a small boat anchorage, is a much nicer environment than the industrial harbor in Victoria, and partly because of the exceptional friendliness of the harbor police who administer the check-in formalities. "Please sign our guest book and look at our photographs," was their first request after we arrived. The guest book was full of testimonials to the excellent treatment previous yachts had experienced at the hands of our hosts, together with photographic mementos of their visits. One recent picture showed a policeman proudly standing with the crew of a visiting boat, and holding an enormous dead king cobra by the tail. "Where did you find that?" I asked, impressed. "We caught it in his engine room," he replied nonchalantly—as if cornering deadly reptiles on pleasure boats was a regular occurrence, and all part of a day's work.

He explained what had happened, and later we were able to confirm his story when we met the boat and its captain in Kuching. The snake was discovered slithering around the engine room by one of the crew. She wisely backed off (ran like hell might be a more accurate description), and the owner called the police. After a long and cautious search that must have been above and beyond the call of duty, the poisonous visitor was finally cornered, and enticed into a sack. "How did it get into the boat in the first place?" I asked, anxious to make sure MOONSHINER remained a snake-free zone. "It must have crawled into the dinghy when they came ashore, and then hid in the bilge or under a seat," suggested the policeman. "We're not sure how it got from the dinghy into the boat. Maybe they hauled the dinghy on deck, or maybe it climbed up the anchor line." I looked at the picture of the seven-foot snake again—dinghy excursions ashore would never be quite the same, especially at night.

Our departure for Kuching, the capital of Sarawak, a few days later was hopefully witnessed by very few observers. The harbor entrance channel is marked by a long line of large buoys that extend out to sea for a considerable distance. It was a calm day, and not a breath of wind rippled the surface of the sea as we motored out under a cloudless sky. I think it was boredom that must have prompted me to say to Lot "If I look backwards, and line up a couple of these buoys, I'll be able to tell if there's any current running." I faced the stern, carefully lined up the row of buoys behind MOONSHINER, and held a straight course, looking for any sign of the current pushing us sideways. "There's no current at all, the buoys are still exactly in line," I informed Lot. As if to maliciously prove the point, at that moment there was a loud crash as we ploughed headlong into the buoy ahead—which was also exactly in line. I looked at Lot, who rolled her eyes and shook her head. The mark of truly great crew is that they know when to shut up.

Kuching

Kuching lies about 18 miles from the open sea, on the banks of the Sarawak River. In 1839 an English adventurer, James Brooke, arrived in the region aboard his yacht, the ROYALIST. Sarawak, at the time, was a principality controlled by the Sultan of Brunei, who requested Brooke's help in quelling outbreaks of violence against his rule. Brooke took full advantage of the situation, and in return for his assistance he was installed as the local Sultan. Brooke further strengthened his position, and in 1842 he took over the province as the first "White Rajah" of Sarawak, and founded a family dynasty that ruled the country for 100 years. His son, Charles, built many of the buildings that still line the waterfront, where MOONSHINER dropped anchor next to PAX.

Like most visiting yachts we anchored near the riverbank in the center of the city, close to a large golden mosque. The next morning we began a day long check-in process that involved visiting three or four government offices in different parts of the town. "Welcome to Kuching and please stay as long as you want," said the customs officer as he stamped our papers. The waterfront was a maze of small shops and fascinating alleyways, and close to the anchorage there was an excellent food market where inexpensive fresh vegetables, fruit, and spices of all kinds were available. Rather than take the dinghy ashore, we found it easier to hail one of the small boats that ferry people back and forth across the river.

The Kuching River flowed rapidly, and tangled islands of floating vegetation and small logs were swept continuously downstream by the current—evidence of the deforestation that was taking place in the interior. From time to time branches became snagged on the anchor cable, and once this happened more flotsam was soon added to the pile. Once the process started it didn't take long before a small floating forest was pushing against MOONSHINER's bow. A telltale humming noise from the anchor chain, as it began to vibrate under the increasing pressure, usually warned us of the problem. This happened once or twice each day, and the only solution was to work from the bow of the boat or the dinghy, and break up the jam using an oar or a boat hook. Local people told us that the problem was getting worse, and that excessive logging up-river had denuded the hillsides, leading to more frequent flooding and an increase in floating debris downstream.

Very early one morning, soon after our arrival, we were still in our bunks when I heard sounds coming from outside the hull, near the bow. I got up to investigate. One of the skippers who ferry people across the river had noticed debris building up on our anchor chain, and had taken the trouble to row over and clear it away. He was removing the last remnants as I came on deck. I thanked him. But he just smiled, and waved goodbye as he headed back across the river in the early morning light in search of passengers. This happened on several different occasions, and with different ferry boats: if they saw debris building up on our bow, or thought we were having trouble clearing it away, they would row over to help, and then leave with a smile and a wave.

After ten days in Kuching, we headed back down the Sarawak River, and anchored for the night in a small quiet tributary half way to the sea. The surrounding riverbank was covered with a dense tall growth of thick vegetation that looked like sugar cane. The following day we continued our journey downstream, and then spent a rather rolly night at anchor, just outside the river mouth, before heading for a midday rendezvous with PAX at Satang Besar, a beautiful and isolated island ten miles further west.

After playing with Fluke on the beach, late in the afternoon we collected dry coconut husks (which make great barbecue fuel), lit a fire, and cooked dinner as we watched the sun set into a golden ocean, and drank red wine under a sky that came alive with stars. Later, as we sat around the fire, chatting, Lot became quiet and then said "Listen, I think the surf's getting up." We stopped talking, and sure enough, the sound of waves breaking on the beach was unmistakable, and we noticed for the first time that an onshore wind had developed over our side of the small island. It was pitch dark as we walked to the water's edge to take a look. A couple of hours earlier there had been scarcely a ripple on the water, but now there were two-foot breaking waves. "Let's get out of here before we have to swim," I said prophetically, as we quickly began collecting our belongings. Frances and Michel left first, and immediately disappeared into the darkness. Lot got in the front of our dinghy, and I gave a push from the stern. We were clear of the beach, and almost through the surf, when a wave caught us at a bad angle, and the next thing I knew we were in the water, underneath the boat.

We managed to turn it the right way up, and climbed back aboard while retrieving the plastic bag that contained our belongings. Not surprisingly, our swamped outboard refused to start again, and I had a hard row against the waves to reach MOONSHINER, anchored a couple of hundred yards offshore. It was an unnerving experience, and we vowed to be more careful in future when partying ashore. The next day we sailed to the anchorage at Datu Point, our last stop in Sarawak. And the following morning we headed out into the China Sea, bound for Aur Island—our landfall near the Malay Peninsula, 300 miles to the west.

The Malay Peninsula

It was almost nine o'clock, on our third night at sea, when I came on watch and Lot pointed out a row of lights directly ahead that looked like fishing boats. "They seem really close," she said. "We'd better be careful. I'll stay up for a while." Since leaving Hong Kong we'd become reasonably proficient at keeping out of the way of fishing boats, which isn't always as easy as it sounds, especially at night. They often work in groups, towing long nets and making repeated course changes; no sooner would we think we had safely passed, than they'd change course and maneuver back in front of us. With our radar out of action it was also difficult to judge their exact distance, so we normally gave them a wide berth.

We continued on our course towards the lights, but as time went by I was puzzled that they didn't seem to be getting any closer. There were dozens of them, some were heading north and others, further away, were heading south towards Singapore. Then I realized what I was looking at. "They aren't nearby fishing boats at all," I said to Lot. "They're big freighters, probably 15 miles away, following the Singapore traffic lanes." It was a strange optical illusion. The boats seemed so close, and it was only the length of time it was taking for us to reach them that indicated their real distance. Later, as we got closer, freighter after freighter marched across our path in silent succession, making us feel like a small turtle trying to cross a busy highway.

At three o'clock that morning we were clear of the shipping lanes and only a couple of miles from our destination. We hove-to and waited for dawn, rather than risk approaching the unfamiliar anchorage in the dark. As the first glimmer of daylight began to lighten the sky we resumed our course, and a couple of hours later we were safely at anchor. "Time for breakfast," said Lot as she put the coffee on the stove. It had been a busy and stressful night, and neither of us had got much sleep. We ate a hearty breakfast, and then slept for the rest of the morning.

Head Hunters of Borneo

Head hunting has a long and honorable history amongst the indigenous people of Borneo's interior, the Dayaks. They believed that at birth everyone was endowed with a body, a mind, and several souls. One group, the Iban, believed that one of these souls resided in a person's head. By taking an enemy's head a warrior achieved not only great status within his tribe, but he also acquired the victim's soul, along with his strength and power.

For the whole village, the taking of heads was an important ritual that pleased the spirits, and guaranteed divine assistance in crucial matters—such as deciding where to plant crops, guaranteeing a good harvest, and assuring protection against enemies.

After successful head hunting expeditions, great celebrations greeted the returning warriors. The brains were extracted through the nostrils, and the skull was then smoke-cured over fires. The heads were treated with great respect, and placed in a *head house* next to the village's communal *long house*. The dried skulls were believed to be a source of great magic, which would continue to benefit the village, and heads were often surrounded by palm leaves and offered food, so that their spirits would forgive what had happened and accept their new home. Some tribes believed that the power of a head increased over time, and valued skulls were handed down from generation to generation. Other tribes, the kind you didn't want as neighbors, considered that a skull's power declined with age, and the welfare of the village demanded that fresh heads be acquired on a regular basis. A village without heads was considered weak and vulnerable.

The tradition of head-hunting was inextricably linked with the Dayak art of tattooing. Tattoos were not made for aesthetic reasons, but as an expression of a person's religious and cultural identity. Obtaining a tattoo was a spiritual act that was used to mark significant events in a villager's life, or to celebrate important rites of passage. In men, tattooing was normally associated with participation in a headhunt. and was a visible sign of the warrior's success. In women, it typically marked a coming of age. Tattoos also represented the social standing of a particular group within the community, and designs were often passed on from one generation to the next.

A combination of objections by Dutch colonialists and Christian missionary zeal led to a steep decline in head-hunting practices towards the end of the nineteenth century. There was a brief resurgence during World War II, when allied forces encouraged the practice—as long as it was directed against Japanese troops. More recently, distorted echoes of the old ways have resurfaced in ethnic riots in Kalimantan, where Dayaks have attacked and beheaded Madurese settlers that the Indonesian government sent as migrants into the region. More than four hundred people were recently slaughtered, and many of the bodies were decapitated. But the motivation reflected ethnic hatred rather than the traditional goal of assuaging the spirits and seeking protection for the village.

11. Breakdown

Tioman broke clear of the haze, its twin-peaked mountain rising majestically out of the ocean, the summit shrouded in a white cap of misty cloud. It is the most famous island off Malaysia's east coast, and its gorgeous beaches became familiar to millions of movie fans who enjoyed Hollywood's musical blockbuster *South Pacific*, and thought they were admiring the legendary beauty of the islands in the South Seas. In fact the film was shot on location at the equally romantic Tioman, and the setting was the South China Sea.

We made our landfall in Tekek Bay on the northwest coast of the island, and dropped anchor in 50 feet of crystal clear water. We chose an area of sandy bottom to avoid damaging the coral heads, and after several attempts we finally persuaded our anchor to take a grudging hold. Many of the anchorages that are considered safe in Southeast Asia would be downright dangerous if they were located in higher latitudes. What makes the difference is the consistency of the monsoon winds—which blow reliably from the northeast during the winter months and from the southwest in the summer. But in addition to the poor holding of its sandy bottom, Tekek Bay was also open to the west, which exposed it to the prevailing summer monsoon. So after a few nights spent worrying that MOONSHINER was about to drag her anchor, we decided to move. By then Frances and Michel had arrived on PAX, and so we set off together hoping to find a less rolly anchorage on the sheltered side of the island in Juara Bay, where the movie had been filmed.

We were motorsailing around the top of the island, when I noticed the engine's temperature gauge was unusually high. We tried slowing down, but it didn't seem to make any difference. "We'd better stop the engine altogether before we do some serious damage," I said to Lot. So we sailed the rest of the way to the anchorage, where I set to work to find the cause of the problem. After checking the obvious possibilities, such as a blocked water inlet or clogged filters, I finally bit the bullet and stripped the water pump itself—but I still couldn't find anything wrong. I cleaned and reassembled the parts, and then restarted the engine. Everything looked fine for a couple of minutes, and then the temperature gauge started to go off the scale. I let the engine run on low revs while I tried to figure out what was wrong. Apart from the high temperature it sounded normal, and it seemed to be running smoothly. Then my heart sank. "My God, the piston isn't moving." The water pump in our old Yanmar is driven directly off the engine's camshaft. The pump assembly is mounted on the outside of the engine and easily accessible, but it's powered by a piston that disappears into the bowels of the 940 lb. monster and is totally inaccessible. It must have been working intermittently, and now it had packed up altogether. We had a major problem.

The only chance of getting the engine back into action was to find a specialist diesel mechanic, preferably one who was familiar with old Yanmars. It came as no surprise to discover that no such person existed on Tioman. We were told our best hope was to take MOONSHINER to Mersing, a fishing port on the mainland coast 30 miles to the southwest. The only problem was that the town was surrounded by barely submerged mudflats which extended well offshore. The entrance was narrow and winding, with a dredged channel that was barely deep enough for shallow draft fishing boats; at high tide it had a charted depth of just over two meters. MOONSHINER's draft is a fraction under two meters, so getting safely into the harbor in a choppy sea was going to be an interesting exercise. We arranged a tow from Tioman with a local boat whose skipper claimed to know the Mersing harbor entrance like the back of his hand. The cost was US$500, an astronomical amount by local standards, but there was no way we could have negotiated the twisting entrance under sail—and if we wanted a tow, he was the only game in town.

He arrived at six in the morning, and Lot and I took turns steering throughout the day. Our early start was designed so that our arrival would be timed to coincide with high tide. The weather co-operated with a light wind and fairly calm sea, and seven hours after leaving Tioman we entered the river, on schedule. We made it into the harbor, but only just: our depth sounder regularly gave readings that indicated we had less than a foot of water under the keel. At times we could sense that MOONSHINER was scraping the muddy bottom as we struggled to stay exactly behind our tow.

Mersing

With a sigh of relief we tied up to the outermost end of a long float, which projected far out from the riverbank. It was the deepest water we could find, but we had only three feet of clearance under the keel, and at low tide MOONSHINER sat firmly on the bottom. Our towboat captain went to call for a mechanic, while we took in our new surroundings. Mersing was a colorful town, with a sizeable fleet of gaily painted fishing boats moored in rows along both banks of the river. MOONSHINER attracted a lot of attention from fishermen and people passing by; the sight of a visiting sailboat was obviously a rarity, thanks to the harbor's intimidating entrance. I wasn't looking forward to the prospect of navigating our own way back to the open sea, but for the time being we had more immediate problems to worry about.

Within an hour of our arrival a mechanic came aboard, and

introduced himself as Mr. Ong. I explained the problem, and while he was examining the engine Lot and I went back to the cockpit to discuss our options. In a worst-case scenario we knew we could bring in a mechanic from Singapore, but we shuddered to think of the cost. Frankly, we were skeptical that anyone in Mersing would be able to make the necessary repairs, and even if they could we were sure it would require the hair-raising removal of the heavy engine from the boat.

In the middle of our morbid speculation Mr. Ong returned, smiling. "No problem," he said, with an easy confidence we didn't yet share. "It's too late to start today, but I'll be back in the morning." "Do we need to take the engine out of the boat?" I asked, afraid that I already knew the answer. "Not necessary to take the engine out," he replied. It sounded too good to be true. "Do you know this type of engine?" I asked, still wondering if he knew what he was getting into. He smiled again and pointed to a row of fishing boats tied up on the other side of the river. "All those boats have your engine, exactly the same," he said. It seems that half the small fishing boats in Southeast Asia used our brand of engine. That was the first piece of good news. The second piece, although we didn't know it yet, was that we'd just met the best mechanic ever to work on our boat.

It took Mr. Ong two days to complete the work, and he spent most of that time working on his back in our shoebox of an engine room. Calling it a room is to give it a distinction it doesn't deserve; sandwiched between the companionway and our tiny rear cabin, it provides 18 inches of clearance on each side of the engine, and has a headroom of less than three feet. Staying in there long enough to carry out an oil change guarantees a visit to the local chiropractor. But despite the horrendous working conditions, he managed to extract the broken piston and replace it by dismantling the gearbox. When it was all over, he presented us with a bill for $120 dollars, including parts. We were embarrassed at how little he charged, and gave him a tip big enough to compensate for the real value of his work.

We enjoyed Mersing, and after the repairs were completed

we decided to stay a few days longer, and explore the town more thoroughly. And it was during this time that we became friendly with Abdul Ghafar, his wife and three children. Abdul first came to visit the day after our arrival. He was just passing by, but when he saw the boat, and learned that we had broken down, he stopped to ask if he could do anything to help. We thanked him for his offer, but said we had everything we needed. "I will come back tomorrow," he said. "So if you discover you need something, please let me know." We said we would, not expecting to see him again. But the next morning he returned, accompanied by his wife, and once more offered to help. "We are Muslims and the Koran tells us that we should help visitors, so please let us know if there's anything we can do," he explained. We again promised we would, and the next day he and his wife came back again, this time accompanied by their three children. After that they visited us several more times, always anxious to make sure that we were all right, and ask if we needed supplies. When we finally left, they presented us with a small, inscribed wooden vase as a memento of our visit. It still sits on MOONSHINER's navigation table.

We waited for a suitably high tide before venturing back into the twisting river channel. All went well until we hit the wake of a fishing boat that was heading in the opposite direction. As we fell into the trough we hit the bottom with a sickening crash, and not for the first time were we grateful that MOONSHINER's hull is made of steel. The sea was rougher than when we entered the harbor, and on a couple more occasions we felt the boat hit the bottom, but the blows were less violent— cushioned perhaps by the soft mud. We were well over a mile from the harbor entrance before the water became deep enough for us to relax, and a little while later we dropped the anchor about a mile and a half offshore. After a safe but rolly night, we headed north to resume our exploration of Tioman and other nearby islands.

One of our favorite spots was the island of Sembilan, which was joined to its neighbor, Sribuat, by a shallow reef that provided excellent protection from the southwesterly wind and swell. On our first visit we approached the island in a 25-knot squall, but on entering the anchorage we discovered that the water was flat calm. "Maybe we can finally get a decent night's sleep for a change," I said to Lot. We never really got used to the endless rolling which seemed to plague most of the local anchorages. When it was really bad we found the best solution was to sleep sideways—across our cabin—rather than in a fore and aft position. That way, although our head and feet pitched up and down we didn't roll from side to side, and it was at least possible to get some sleep. It was the endless need to brace ourselves, to prevent our bodies from rolling sideways, that kept us awake at night.

Sembilan and Sribuat were uninhabited, perhaps because much of the foreshore was covered with inaccessible mangrove, and guarded by a shallow fringing reef. We spent several idle days exploring the islands with Michel and Frances—swimming, snorkeling, and paddling our dinghies through watery passes in the mangroves. We even discovered a deserted beach, where Lot found a giant clamshell that was well over a foot in diameter.

Every evening local fishing boats dropped anchor between the islands, obviously well aware that the bay would provide an undisturbed night's sleep. One evening Lot rowed over to one of them to ask if she could buy a fish. They immediately gave her one of their biggest, and refused to accept any payment. She rowed back to MOONSHINER for a T-shirt, which she finally persuaded them to accept, in exchange for their gift. Their generosity was typical of the friendliness of almost all the fishermen we met in Asia. But it's also true that piracy is alive and well in the region, and these modern predators no longer come over the horizon flying the skull and cross-bones flag to advertise their intentions. And unfortunately, a tiny minority of fishermen are not averse to joining the profession if an easy opportunity presents itself.

The challenge is to remain vigilant to the possibility that an unknown boat might pose a threat, without becoming paranoid and starting to see Blackbeard the Pirate lurking in every wheel-house. The vast majority of people who make their living from the sea feel a kinship with the sailor willing to take his small boat across an ocean. And far from being a threat, they will embarrass you with their hospitality if you give them half a chance.

12. Singapore

To Lot's disgust, one of my first priorities in Singapore was to head to a downtown Burger King restaurant, and get my first fast food fix in months by devouring a Whopper Burger, complete with large fries and a milkshake. She has always had a greater affinity than I do for Asian food, and visions of deliciously greasy french fries with ketchup had been haunting my dreams for weeks. Our arrival in the city had also been eagerly anticipated by Lot, but for different reasons. Her sister lived there, married to a Singapore Airlines captain, and as they hadn't seen each other for a long time it would give them the chance to catch up on some long overdue family gossip. I also knew Singapore quite well, from my days traveling with Canadian Airlines, so for both of us it was a chance to relax for a while in a familiar environment.

We anchored for a few days in front of the Changi Yacht Club, which has a well-deserved reputation for hospitality towards visiting boats. But the anchorage area was crowded, so we decided to move a few miles further west to a quieter location off Ponggol Point, where we tied up to a mooring buoy next to our old friend Graeme. Ponggol is a small promontory in Johor Strait—the narrow channel that separates the city-state of Singapore from the southern tip of the Malay Peninsula. We had only been there a couple of days when our first Sumatra wind came to visit. These infamous squalls take their name from the Indonesian island to the northwest where they first develop as thunderheads, before heading down Malacca Strait towards Singapore. We had already been warned to be on our guard, but as we figured we were already experienced at handling tropical thunderstorms we hadn't given them much thought.

We were sitting in the cabin when it struck without warning. There was a sound like an approaching express train, and then it was on us. We held onto the furniture as MOONSHINER heeled as if she'd been hit by a truck. I scrambled to the hatch and looked out from behind the protection of the cockpit cover. The visibility was almost zero, and it was impossible to tell if the horizontal bullets of water flying past the boat came from the clouds or were blown off the sea; everything was a grey blur of driven rain and foam. One moment there hadn't been a breath of wind, and the next we had a steady 50-knot that was doing its best to etch the paint off the hull. "I thought we were supposed to get some sort of warning if a Sumatra is expected," said Lot. "So did I," I replied. "I guess someone forget to tell the storm."

Sumatras are often preceded by a distinctive low dark cumulonimbus cloud, which normally gives about an hour's warning. But if there was one, we certainly didn't see it. And conventional wisdom also says that the wind in a Sumatra normally doesn't exceed 30 to 40 knots—so I think we must have been in an acceleration zone, where it picked up speed as it passed through Johor Strait. Either that, or it was just a particularly feisty specimen. If the mooring buoy had started to drag I don't think there's anything we could have done about it, except throw an anchor over the side and hope for the best. Even with our engine on full revs, we would still have been driven backwards onto the nearby shore by the onslaught. But fortunately everything held fast, and the wind soon lost its initial ferocity.

Despite the occasional squall, the only member of MOONSHINER's crew who didn't enjoy Singapore was Fluke, who was banished to the quarantine kennels while we hauled the boat to clean and antifoul the bottom. This turned into an expensive proposition, as she had to be transported in the quarantine department's van and escorted by the resident veterinarian. We also had to rent one of their transportation crates. This example of bureaucracy gone mad cost US$200 each way, for a ten-minute trip. At the kennels they wouldn't accept her Hong Kong vaccination papers, and insisted on giving her the shots again, which added even more to the cost. I understand the importance of keeping rabies off the island, but such excessive charges are counterproductive as they only encourage visiting boats to hide their animals. But at least the quarantine kennels were clean and reasonably spacious, and Fluke was well cared for during her stay. Lot visited her every day, and counted down the days impatiently until she could bring her home.

A couple of days before MOONSHINER was due to be hauled out of the water, we moved to another anchorage that was closer to the boatyard. The crowded bay was packed with boats of all types, and filled with an impressive forest of tall aluminum masts atop a large contingent of modern sailboats. We found space to anchor next to an old wooden sloop that looked dwarfed and out of place surrounded by its larger and more modern neighbors. Shortly after we arrived, the owners rowed over to MOONSHINER to ask if we would be willing to use our dinghy to tow them to a nearby dock, where they'd arranged to have their broken engine repaired.

"I hope this is the last expense for a while," said one of the men as we helped him tie up. "The engine's almost new, and already it's giving us problems. And that's on top of having to replace all our electronic gear last week." "What was wrong with your electronics?" I asked, suspecting that if they were as old as the boat they must have died of old age. "Hit by lightning right here in the harbor," he replied. We were amazed. His mast was made of wood, and at least ten feet shorter than the average height of the surrounding aluminum masts. Yet somehow his neighbors had escaped unscathed, while he'd received a direct hit that cooked every piece of electronic equipment on his boat. I shook my head as I looked up at his rigging. "I know, it's unbelievable but it happened," he said. "We even lost a portable radio that was lying in a drawer." I thought again of our thunderstorms 40 miles off the Philippine coast—when our aluminum mast was the highest thing for miles around, and we were surrounded by repeated lightning strikes that never touched us. If anyone ever figures these things out, please let me know.

A few days later I woke up in the middle of the night feeling nauseated. As I lifted my head off the pillow, the cabin performed a series of wild gyrations that just didn't want to stop. I lay down again and closed my eyes, and after a while the dizziness diminished enough for me to risk climbing down the ladder to the ground. I headed quickly to the bathroom at the other end of the boatyard—an urgent necessity as MOON-SHINER was sitting high and dry in the marina while we worked on repainting her hull, and so our marine head, which flushes with seawater, was out of action.

As I climbed down the ladder another wave of nausea hit me. The world spun, and I was violently sick. "I'm calling a taxi to take you to the hospital," said Lot. "We need to get this checked out." I wasn't sure if I could last the length of the taxi journey without being sick again, but I was feeling so wretched that I didn't put up much of an argument. At the hospital's emergency unit I was given some form of anti-nausea medication and put on a stretcher in a small cubicle, where I was regularly checked—presumably to see if I was still breathing. As the night wore on I gradually felt more human, and in the morning I was given a box of pills and discharged with an inconclusive diagnosis of "non-specific vertigo" and an admonition to "see a doctor if it returns."

On the way back to the boat we tried to figure out what might have caused the attack. My first assumption was that I had eaten something that had violently disagreed with me. But Lot and I had eaten the same dinner, and she had no symptoms. Then I realized it might have been caused by the extremely toxic commercial antifouling paint that I'd been using to paint

MOONSHINER's bottom. It was supposed to be effective against marine growth for five years, and instructions on the container warned of health hazards if it wasn't applied correctly. In North America and Europe, environmental laws prevent the sale of toxic commercial paint for use on recreational boats. There are good reasons for this regulation, but our more cynical boating friends swear that recreational paint is so ineffective that barnacle eat it as a nutritional supplement.

I had no recurrence of vertigo, and true to the product's advertising blurb no barnacles ventured anywhere near our hull for the next few years; I guess they were just too nauseated to hang on.

Piracy

In the early years of the twentieth century, a freighter left Singapore and headed into the South China Sea. The following night the vessel's young captain came onto the bridge to find it deserted, except for the officer of the watch, who was lying unconscious on the floor and bleeding from a head wound. He left the bridge to investigate, and soon came across the prostrate body of his first officer who had also been attacked and beaten unconscious. Moments later he suffered the same fate himself. When he came to, the pirates were long gone and he counted himself lucky to be alive and still in command of his vessel. The story, which was told to me years after the event by one of the captain's friends, wasn't unusual—and the problem still continues today. Piracy has been a way of life in the waters of the South China Sea, the Java Sea, and Malacca Strait for over a thousand years. And the British Navy was still mounting operations against them well into the 1920s.

The threat of pirate attack has always been especially great for shipping in Malacca Strait and its approaches. A 500-mile-long, funnel-shaped waterway between the island of Sumatra and the Malay Peninsula, the Strait is the second busiest commercial waterway in the world; over 600 vessels, from pleasure craft to mammoth freighters, ply its waters every day. Although it is 200 miles wide in the north, it narrows to only 11 miles in the south near Singapore, and pirates have long taken advantage of this bottleneck to pounce on their victims. In ancient times Malay and Sumatran pirates controlled the Indian Ocean side of the Strait. And in the Philippine and Indonesian archipelagos to the east, various aggressive tribes viewed piracy as a legitimate way of life, and terrorized the eastern approaches to the Strait and the waters of the South China Sea. Amongst the most feared predators were the Ilanun from the Philippines, who raided shipping far out into the South China Sea, often to procure prisoners for the slave markets of Sumatra and Java.

In the early nineteenth century the Sea Dayaks of Borneo emerged as the most feared pirates in the area, and in 1836 a Royal Navy squadron was based in Singapore and charged with the task of eliminating the problem once and for all. They had considerable success, and by the second half of the century the incidence of piracy had been reduced, but certainly not eradicated. Ships sailing between Europe and China remained particularly vulnerable, as they had to run the gauntlet of pirates for over 1,000 miles—down the length of Malacca Strait, and then across the South China Sea past the pirates' island-havens in Borneo and the Indonesian archipelago. In the 1840s another threat emerged when a Chinese pirate named Shap Ng Tsai rose to become leader of a fleet of over 70 vessels based at Tin Pak, 170 miles west of Hong Kong. They attacked and captured British and American vessels, and began extorting protection money from traders. Despite numerous attempts to stamp out piracy in Asia, it still persists as a dangerous threat to pleasure craft and commercial vessels alike. And there are indications that in the twenty-first century the problem is getting worse.

Modern Piracy

In November 1998 the bulk carrier CHEUNG HO was carrying a cargo of slag from Shanghai to Malaysia when it was intercepted by pirates just outside Hong Kong waters. All 23 crew members were brutally murdered, and their bodies weighted and thrown overboard. The first evidence of the crime appeared several days later when a number of the corpses became snagged in fishermen's nets. After the murders, the vessel was sold to unknown foreign interests for US$300,000. A Chinese court later sentenced 13 gang members to death, and gave 18 others sentences of up to life in prison for the attack. The case highlighted the increasing incidence of violence and murder associated with pirate attacks, and the close relationship between the pirate gangs and members of the economic and political elite in some Asian countries bordering the South China Sea.

The attack on the CHEUNG HO was carried out by a Chinese gang masquerading as smuggling police, who boarded their victim from an official-looking boat that had previously been used for customs inspections. The individual who provided the gang with the boat and clothing was amongst those later sentenced to death. The gang leader was on the payroll of a wealthy Indonesian businessman of Chinese descent—a billionaire with close friends amongst Indonesia's political and business establishment. Such influential connections are not uncommon, and are one of the major obstacles to combating piracy in Southeast Asia. Many officials are willing to collude with the pirates and profit from their activities, and governments have typically turned a blind eye to the problem. As a result, piracy against international shipping has tripled in the last ten years, and scores of seamen have lost their lives.

In a typical, commando style attack at least 10 men in high-speed boats follow a freighter, and then board it from the stern, usually at night. The crew are overpowered, robbed, and then forced to open the ship's safe, which normally contains thousands of dollars in petty cash. In other attacks the crew are immediately killed or set adrift, and the entire ship is stolen, repainted, given a new name and false papers, and then sold, along with its cargo. Piracy on this scale is the work of highly sophisticated and well-financed international criminal gangs. But smaller scale attacks are also increasing; the victims are usually coastal fishermen or the occasional cruising yacht caught in the wrong place at the wrong time. Occasionally fishermen *are* the pirates, but this is unusual and the predators are more likely to be gangs from local villages where piracy has been a way of life for generations. The best protection for visiting yachts is to talk to the locals and find out what areas to avoid. The dangerous regions are often very localized: the northeast coast of Sabah and the waters south of Mindanao were a *no-go* zone when we sailed through the area in the early 90s, but the western coasts of the Philippines and Borneo were relatively safe.

Not all attacks are made by criminal gangs. Many—perhaps a lot—are carried out by naval, customs, or marine police units operating as privateers with the tacit approval of their superiors. Governments often rationalize this criminal behavior as "excessive zeal" on the part of local commanders in their pursuit of smugglers. The problem is particularly bad in Indonesia, where piracy has flourished with the recent collapse of the economy. It was a common joke amongst sailors we met in Asia that far from helping to solve the problem, Indonesian patrol boats *were* the problem. And during the 1990s many victims of piracy in the South China Sea reported they were attacked by gunboats carrying uniformed Chinese crews. In a rare case of successful prosecution, members of the Philippine Coast Guard illegally seized a Japanese merchant ship in 1995, and were subsequently convicted of robbery in Manila.

In addition to the increasing use of violence, a sinister danger that worries marine safety experts is the possibility that terrorism will become linked to piracy. Al Qaeda and its affiliates have the potential to inflict enormous damage on maritime trade. Half the world's commerce passes through Malacca Strait, including two-thirds of its oil and liquefied natural gas. In a recent attack on a chemical tanker, 10 pirates boarded the vessel, captured the crew, and began navigating the ship. Using these techniques, a freighter carrying dangerous chemical or explosive petroleum products could be used like the aircraft in the 9/11 attack on New York. Eighty percent of the oil imported by Japan, South Korea and China passes through the Strait of Malacca on its way from the Gulf. If terrorists closed the Strait, these oil shipments would be faced with an expensive thousand-mile detour around Sumatra that could lead to a crisis in world oil markets and the global economy.

13. The Pirate Strait

Hundreds of small sailing vessels pass unmolested through the Strait of Malacca each year, despite the waterway's reputation as the most dangerous area for piracy in the world. As the volume of attacks against big commercial vessels increases, perhaps there is less interest in plundering the small fry. Or perhaps they've been lucky. Or chosen the right route: the Malaysian side of the Strait is considered to be much safer than sailing in Indonesian waters, and most small boats keep close to the Malaysian shore. This was certainly our strategy, and MOONSHINER anchored every night on the enjoyable 350-mile passage from Singapore to Thailand.

We got a late start the day we left Singapore, and only covered 20 miles before anchoring for the night behind Kukup Island, opposite a small fishing village on the mainland. As we got underway the following morning we failed to notice a row of widely spaced floats supporting a long fishing net in the muddy water. The line wrapped itself around MOONSHINER's propeller shaft and immediately stalled the engine. We had just finished cutting it loose when a very angry fisherman arrived on the scene. Fearing that we had seriously damaged his means of livelihood Lot was feeling guilty. "We're very sorry, but we had no choice but to cut the line. It was the only way to get it off the propeller," she said.

Our visitor wasn't impressed by her expression of regret, no doubt because he didn't understand a word she was saying. If anything he was getting angrier by the minute, until Lot went below and returned with her wallet. When he saw it he immediately calmed down—now we were finally talking his language. And when Lot handed over some money, and he'd counted it, he became positively cheerful. All was forgiven, and he was smiling from ear to ear as he shook our hands enthusiastically before saying goodbye. "How much did you give him?" I asked. I wanted to treat him fairly, but he'd seemed a bit too cheerful to me and his net could easily be repaired. "Fifty US dollars," she answered. "My God, isn't that a bit much, he'll be on the phone to all his cousins between here and the Thai border, and they'll be stringing out all their nets as soon as they see our mast on the horizon." "Don't exaggerate," she said, but with less than her usual conviction.

Malacca

Just over 100 miles north of Singapore, on the western shore of the Malay Peninsula, lies the historic city of Malacca. Its rich and colorful history reflects its strategic location on the maritime route that links China, India, the Middle East, and Europe. For centuries it was a thriving trading hub for silks from China, spices from India and Southeast Asia, and European goods arriving via Cairo and Aden. By the time Zheng He arrived with his first fleet in 1403 it already had a reputation as one of the richest places on earth. But its wealth was a magnet to pirates, as Zheng He soon discovered.

As he approached Malacca on his way to India, Zheng's fleet was attacked by a Chinese pirate from Guangzhou, Chen Zuyi, who had taken control of the nearby Sumatran city of Pelambang. On the outward journey Zheng avoided a full-blown confrontation, perhaps because he was unsure of the enemy's strength, but on his return in 1405 he set about destroying the pirate fleet. Official Chinese histories of the period say that Chen indicated early in the confrontation that he wanted to surrender, but that Zheng rejected the offer when he was informed that it was just a trick. Trick or not, surrender sounds like a sensible idea: faced with the overwhelming size of the Treasure Fleet the eventual outcome of the confrontation could hardly have been in doubt. And the Chinese naval vessels of the period didn't lack for innovative armament, including incendiary weapons that fired burning gunpowder and flaming paper at the enemy's sails to set them ablaze, or gunpowder and paper grenades that were soaked in poison or contained lethal chunks of metal and explosives. Other devices scattered human waste, or discharged smoke-producing chemicals. Maritime battles against the Chinese fleet must have been hot, smelly, and confusing affairs.

It took Zheng several months to finally defeat the pirates by luring them into an ambush near Pelambang, and then burning or capturing a large number of their ships. Chen was taken prisoner and returned to China—where he was later beheaded— and for the next 30 years the city of Malacca became an important base for Chinese expeditions heading west. But with the end of the great Treasure Fleet in 1433, few Chinese boats ventured beyond the Strait and into the Indian Ocean, and Arab ships resumed control of trade to destinations in India, Arabia, and East Africa. However, their dominance didn't last long. Less than 70 years after the last Treasure Fleet returned to China, the Portuguese explorer Vasco da Gama discovered the route to the Indies via South Africa. And a few years later, in 1519, his countryman Magellan led the first expedition to circumnavigate the globe, and reached the Indies via the Pacific.

It is interesting to speculate on how different the future of Europe, and much of the rest of the world, might have been if China had not abandoned its fleet, and the European explorers had run into a Chinese armada of almost 30,000 men in the Indian Ocean in the early years of the sixteenth century. On a historical scale they barely missed each other: a young child watching Zheng He depart Malacca for the last time might also have witnessed, as a very old man or woman, the arrival in the same port of the Portuguese flotilla under Diego Lopez de Sequeira in 1509. But miss each other they did, and two years later, in 1511, Alfonso d'Albuquerque returned with a flotilla of

18 Portuguese ships and proceeded to bombard the city into submission. Europeans quickly extended their influence throughout Africa, Asia, and the Far East, and dominated much of the world for the next 400 years.

Heading North

Thanks to a following current, that at times reached five knots, we made fast progress up Malacca Strait, even though we stopped to anchor each night. And 16 days after leaving Singapore we arrived at the island of Pinang.

The day of our arrival we had made a particularly long run, and didn't reach the island until just after sunset, in a gathering thunderstorm. We were tired, and anxious to find shelter before the storm struck, so after carefully studying the chart we decided to break our rule of not attempting to enter a strange anchorage after dark. It was a serious mistake. "I think the storm's about to hit us," said Lot, just as we were entering a small bay on the island's southeast coast. No sooner had she spoken than the storm broke with a vengeance. In the torrential rain the visibility fell to almost zero. The smart thing to do would have been to turn around, but the anchorage was so close that we were reluctant to head back out.

"If you keep a lookout from the bow, I'll go ahead dead slow," I said to Lot. MOONSHINER crept slowly towards the shore, which was invisible except as a rain-obscured line on the radar screen, while I kept a close eye on the depth sounder. Suddenly Lot shouted in alarm "Look out, a rock." Then I saw it: a smooth black vertical wall rising ten feet out of the water. It was scarcely a boat-length ahead—which gives a good indication of how poor the visibility had become. I threw the engine into reverse and gunned the throttle, and we stopped with only a few feet to spare. We backed off, and waited for the rain to ease up before making a second attempt to approach the shore. This time we made it without incident.

George Town, the major city on Pinang, has established

itself in recent years as the Silicon Valley of Southeast Asia, thanks in large part to the energy and business skills of its ethnic Chinese population. Much of the city is a living museum to its colonial past, and takes its name from the reigning British monarch at the time when its founder, Captain Francis Light, acquired the island from the Sultan of Kedah at the end of the eighteenth century. Amongst the island's many attractions is a ride on the funicular railway to the top of the 2,700-foot summit of Pinang Hill, which commands a magnificent eagle's eye view of the town, and the mainland of the Malay Peninsula in the far distance. Lot and I rode up the hill on the funicular one sunny afternoon, and then decided to walk back to town by following a trail through the forest that covers the hillside.

The winding path was virtually deserted, and the quiet solitude we found amongst the trees was a welcome change from the hustle and bustle of the nearby town. About halfway down the hill we rounded a bend, and came upon an elderly Chinese man who was energetically engrossed in sweeping the path clear of leaves with a large brush. As the entire forest floor was littered with leaves beyond counting, his task seemed akin to trying to empty the world's oceans with a teaspoon. He smiled as we approached, and we stopped to talk. Lot soon asked the obvious question: "Why are you sweeping the forest floor?" "I come here to meditate," he said. "In the forest it is good to meditate. I like it here. I come every day to be in the forest, and to meditate." "Do you meditate by sweeping?" asked Lot, her Dutch pragmatism getting the better of her. "No, no, not by the sweeping, but the forest gives me much pleasure, and I want to give it something back. So I clean its paths."

We talked for some time. He was a delightful and friendly man, and after we said goodbye he went back to his task of "giving something back to the forest." We might easily have dismissed our new friend as just a local eccentric and soon forgotten the incident. But he exuded a quiet joyfulness and contentment that has kept him in our memories ever since. Whenever I mention Pinang, Lot still reacts by saying: "Do you remember the man on the mountain?"

The encounter reminded me of an incident that had occurred the previous year. My final consulting assignment, before leaving the corporate world, had been in the Taiwanese capital of Taipei. My last day on the job had just ended, and as I headed to the airport to catch the flight home for the last time, I found it hard to believe that our sailing dreams were about to come true. It was rush-hour on Friday evening, and at the airport I joined the ranks of hundreds of other preoccupied travelers, all hurrying to get to their flights on time.

As I approached the arrival and departure gates I began to hear the incongruous but hauntingly beautiful sound of a flute. I kept walking, and the music became progressively louder. Soon, I saw that it was coming from an elderly Buddhist monk who was sitting alone at the side of the corridor, totally absorbed in his playing, and oblivious to the tide of stressed humanity rushing past. He had created his own private oasis of calm in the midst of the airport's hurried frenzy, and most people scarcely spared him a passing glance. He behaved as if he was playing in the most peaceful setting on earth—as if he didn't know, or care, that the airport even existed. I paused and listened. After a while he stopped playing, and his face broke into a spontaneous laughing smile as if, despite the surrounding mayhem, he was recalling all the peaceful pleasures that life has to offer. Perhaps he was. Whenever Lot thinks of Pinang she remembers the man in the forest. Whenever I think of Taiwan I remember the monk at the airport. We remember each of them for the same reason.

Magellan at Malacca

Ten years before he would achieve lasting fame as leader of the first expedition to sail around the globe, Ferdinand Magellan was serving in Asia with a Portuguese flotilla under the command of Diego Lopez de Sequeira. On September 11, 1509, they anchored off Malacca, and a delegation from the flotilla met with the local sultan as envoys of the king of Portugal. They signed a peace treaty, and the Portuguese were given permission to begin trading: they were told that a warehouse full of pepper was available, if they would provide the manpower to transport it to the docks. Local Chinese merchants warned the Portuguese that the sultan was plotting a treacherous attack, and a local Malay girl also warned Magellan's closest friend, Francisco Serrão, that skulduggery was afoot, and that Arab merchants had convinced the sultan to capture the lightly defended Portuguese ships while the work party was ashore.

But Sequeira ignored the warnings, and sent off a party of a hundred men, under the command of Serrão, to collect the pepper. While they were ashore a fleet of sampans converged on the Portuguese flotilla under the pretext of wanting to trade. Only a few of the natives were allowed to board the boat on which Magellan was serving. But the vessel's captain, de Sousa, was alarmed to see many more climbing aboard Sequeira's flagship, and despatched Magellan to warn him. Magellan arrived to find Sequeira playing chess with a Malay nobleman, who was surrounded by eight armed guards who were waiting for the order to attack. On being warned of the danger Sequeira immediately ordered the visitors off his ship, and sent his mate aloft to see what was happening ashore.

Signal smoke was coming from the sultan's palace, and a mob on the waterfront had cut off the shore party from their boats. The mate shouted a warning, and when they realized what was happening most of the shore party fled for safety towards the warehouse. But Serrão and a few companions started fighting their way back to the boats. Magellan and two other men hurried ashore in a skiff, recovered one of the longboats, and then held a beachhead long enough for some of the shore party to reach the boats, and then fight their way back to the flotilla through the hostile sampans. Most of the men who had fled towards the warehouse were captured, and many of those who had tried to fight their way back to the waterfront were killed. In total over half the shore party were captured or killed in the incident, and many of the flotilla's captains wanted to bombard the city in retaliation.

But Sequeira refused, and instead he offered a ransom for any men who were still alive. After waiting for two days without receiving a reply he departed Malacca bound for India, worried that the monsoon winds would soon reverse direction. Two years later, Magellan was aboard the flotilla commanded by Albuquerque that returned to Malacca to avenge Sequeira's humiliation. After a bloody siege lasting six weeks, the city was finally captured.

14. Langkawi

Langkawi, and its neighboring islands, sit just south of the border between Malaysia and Thailand, and we arrived to find a flotilla of sailboats already at anchor in front of the small town of Kuah. We dropped our hook on the outside of the fleet, next to our old friend Graeme on NEFERTITI whom we'd last seen in Singapore, and we spent a fine evening swapping stories of our travels up the Strait. But we found the anchorage a bit too crowded for our liking, and a couple of days later we moved to a tiny nook on nearby Gabang Darat Island.

The scenery was as beautiful as the weather. We approached the anchorage under a clear blue sky, through a channel which cut between the two large islands covered with spectacularly shaped rock formations. The passage was flanked by sheer cliffs topped with lush jungle vegetation, and when we arrived at our destination we were delighted to discover we had it all to ourselves— which was just as well as there was scarcely room for even one boat in the almost landlocked bay.

We spent two wonderful days anchored in our private hideaway, where we relaxed, read books, and watched time go by. A couple of times each day I took Fluke for rides in the dinghy around the shoreline, expeditions she always loved. One of the great pleasures of visiting a country by sailboat is that you can reach so many beautiful places that are totally inaccessible by any other means of transport.

We often refer to MOONSHINER as our wooden egg, which may seem a strange epithet for a sailboat made out of steel. But inside, our cabin is finished in warm red cedar, and her floor is beautifully planked with maple and cherry hardwood. Sitting in the comfort of her cozy cabin we feel as protected as chicks inside their eggs, even at sea. She is our private wooden cocoon. And she is willing to take us safely anywhere in the world, whenever we ask her.

Unwanted Guests

We returned to Kuah to top up on supplies before leaving for Thailand. We went ashore with Graeme to do the shopping, and just as we were about to load everything into the dinghies he warned, "Make sure you take everything out of the cardboard boxes and wash all the containers in seawater." "Why? It all looks clean enough," I objected. "Cockroaches," he replied. "The easiest way to become infested with cockroaches is to bring their eggs onboard in grocery containers." "I wish we'd known that earlier," said Lot. "We've been providing a home to several generations of the beasts ever since we left Hong Kong."

Almost all the boats we met sailing in the tropics fought an ongoing battle with cockroach infestation. These tough little critters are one of nature's most successful species, having survived virtually unchanged since the time that dinosaurs roamed the planet. Very few things freak Lot out, but the sight of a cockroach in the cabin when she is sitting quietly reading a book sends her into shrieking fits. We tried all sorts of ways to get rid of them, including setting off the powerful insecticide bombs that are supposed to have enough poison inside them to send an African rhino to the emergency room, but somehow they still managed to survive.

Some varieties have no trouble at all coming aboard, because they can fly. Lot swears that she can easily tell an old timer from a new resident. She often explains to visitors, "If you turn on the light in the middle of the night you usually take them by surprise—running around on the cabin floor. You can recognize the old hands because they immediately run for the nearest escape hole, but the newcomers panic, and run in circles looking for a way out." At this point our non-sailing guests seem to get a strange look on their faces, as if questioning whether a dinner onboard MOONSHINER with the Sparhams is a good idea after all. I normally offer a helpful "Why don't we paint the long-term residents different colors, and then give them names? That way we can treat them like proper members of the family." Oh well, it prevents us having to cook for repeat visitors too often. We didn't get rid of the last cockroach until a bitterly cold winter a couple of years later froze MOONSHINER into the ice in Holland, and killed them all off. But that's another story.

Thailand

Our first landfall in Thailand was in the spectacularly beautiful Butang Islands. We made the short 25-mile hop from Langkawi, in company with NEFERTITI, in a strong northeaster that kicked up a nasty short sea. But in the protected passage between the islands of Ko Ladang and Ko Rawi, the water was calm and crystal clear as we dropped anchor in one of the most beautiful spots MOONSHINER has ever visited. We spent three idyllic days enjoying the deserted beach at Ko Ladang. When we weren't picnicking, snorkeling, or playing with Fluke, we took advantage of a small clean freshwater stream that ran out of the jungle and across the dazzling white sand to bathe, do our washing, and remove the salt from our diving gear. After sunset, pools of light from the squid fishing fleet drifted slowly across the bay and later, when they'd gone, the islands lay silent and still in the warm tropical night beneath a blaze of stars.

Eventually it was time to move on, and we reluctantly hauled up our anchor and headed north towards the town of Phuket, which would be our jumping off point for the 1,000 mile crossing of the Andaman Sea to Sri Lanka.

Phuket Island is one of the world's great rendezvous for the offshore sailing fleet—whose itinerary is never as haphazard as it appears, but is dictated by the timetable of the world's weather patterns. Typhoon and hurricane seasons must be avoided, and full advantage taken of favorable monsoon winds. Whether they plan to continue their voyage via the Red Sea and Mediterranean, or take the southerly route by way of South Africa, many circumnavigators cross paths in Phuket. It is a place where sailors can share stories, and meet new and old friends while preparing their boats for the next ocean crossing. Christmas in Phuket had become a traditional prelude to the annual migration of yachts across the Indian Ocean, which takes place in January with the onset of the winds of the northeast monsoon. The anchorage where most visiting boats congregate, Ao Chalong, is a truly magnificent spot.

On Christmas Day, after dark, a group of cruising sailors were having a beach party in the bay where MOONSHINER was anchored on the west coast of the island. During the festivities, two of them decided to head back to their boat in a dinghy to collect a fresh supply of beer. They were never seen again. The northeast monsoon was blowing off the land at about 25 knots, but the sea close to shore was deceptively calm and they probably never realized the danger they were in. A strong offshore wind is a frequent killer of surfboarders and people in dinghies who develop engine trouble.

"It happens almost every year," said a spokesman for the marine police after they and the coastguard, had given up the search for the missing sailors. "Their outboard engine probably broke down, and they drifted offshore while trying to fix it. They wouldn't notice the waves until they were too far out to get back." It was the deadly simplicity of the tragedy that somehow made it more shocking. Sitting on the protected beach the two men would hardly have been aware that there was any wind blowing at all. And once offshore, the waves would soon have been large enough to swamp their small fiberglass boat.

We couldn't know it at the time, but this same beautiful bay would soon be the site of another Christmas tragedy on a far greater scale. Within a few short years it would be devastated by one of the greatest natural disasters ever to hit the Indian Ocean: the deadly tsunami of December 26, 2004.

Nineteen miles beneath the seabed, 100 miles off the coast of northwest Sumatra, a 1,200-kilometer stretch of the Indian tectonic plate was thrust with unimaginable force 20 meters under its neighbor, the Burma plate. It was just before 8:00 a.m. local time, and the powerful earthquake raised the seafloor along the fault-line by several meters in a matter of seconds. It was the fourth most powerful earthquake in over 100 years, and the resulting tsunami, or tidal wave, would kill almost 300,000 people in the Indian Ocean basin.

In deep water the passage of a tsunami is undetectable. Although it travels at the speed of a jet plane, it is little more than a foot in height, and would not even be noticed as it passed a boat in the open ocean. But when it reaches shallow water friction with the seabed slows it down, and as it slows its height increases. When the wave struck Phuket, less than two hours after the earthquake, its height was estimated at 15 feet. Closer to the epicenter of the earthquake, on the coast of northwest Sumatra, the height of the tidal wave is believed to have been at least 10 meters and probably much more.

Along the west coast of Thailand over 11,000 people, visitors and local residents, are believed to have died. But this figure almost pales in comparison with the more than 240,000 people who perished closer to the quake's epicenter along the coast of Sumatra. A tragedy of this scale is impossible to comprehend, and the suffering of the survivors in the stricken areas continues as they try to rebuild shattered lives and earn enough to support themselves and their families. In Phuket, six months after the wave struck, few tourists had returned and thousands of people remained unemployed.

15. The Bay of Bengal

MOONSHINER pointed her bow towards the sunset, and the vague outline of Phuket Island gradually grew fainter until it finally disappeared astern. Ahead, across more than 1,000 miles of ocean, lay our next landfall, the ancient port city of Galle, in Sri Lanka. Neither Lot nor I felt much like talking as we sat together in the cockpit as darkness fell. We felt very much alone. This was only our second major offshore passage since leaving Hong Kong, and the first we would make by ourselves. I was feeling tense, preoccupied with thoughts of how far we had to sail, and the knowledge that we only had our own resources to rely on in an emergency.

Earlier in the day we'd said a final goodbye to Graeme, who was heading back to Singapore on NEFERTITI. He had vast sailing experience in Southeast Asia, and we'd benefited enormously from his helpful advice. In the nine months since we met in Kota Kinabalu we'd become good friends, and we were sad in the unspoken understanding that we probably wouldn't see him again. Now, as we sat lost in our own thoughts, our spirits weren't improved by the fact that there was no moon, and the watery world around us was as black as pitch. Suddenly, Lot let out a shout: "Look, dolphins."

Within seconds we were surrounded by flashing bullets of phosphorescence, as a dozen of these friendly visitors sped towards the boat and then kept pace with us, diving under the keel and playing tag with the bow wave. We had often appreciated the company of visiting dolphins, but they were never more welcome than on this first night of our passage to Sri Lanka. Lot later told a friend, "At the beginning I was apprehensive, but as soon as I saw the dolphins I knew that everything was going to be OK. It was as if they were saying *'don't worry, everything's alright so come and play with us, come and play'.*"

Dolphins always seem to arrive with no motive other than to play, and show off around the boat out of sheer exuberance, and their company never fails to raise our spirits. When Fluke is below deck she seems to know when they're coming, long *before* they actually arrive, presumably because she hears the high-pitched sounds they emit. Then she runs excitedly to the bow, and barks at them as they sport around the boat. But on this occasion she was wearing her safety harness, and could only watch them from the security of the cockpit. We have a rule that nobody, including Fluke, is allowed on deck at night unless they're attached to the boat.

We were 200 miles from our destination, and traveling at hull-speed under full sail, when MOONSHINER was brought to a halt in a bone-jarring crash; we'd fallen off a wave onto a massive log, floating invisibly just below the surface. I dove under the forepeak to check for damage with my heart pounding. "I don't see anything," I shouted back to Lot. "Thank God for steel," she said. We hove-to and checked the boat carefully, but despite the violence of the impact we couldn't see any damage.

As we approached the southeast tip of Sri Lanka, we were hit by a powerful thunder squall that packed the strongest winds we experienced during the passage. Spray swept the boat as I turned on the deck lights and went forward to put an extra reef in the main. The storm didn't last long enough for the waves to build to any significant height, although it was exciting enough while it lasted. But later that same day we had a much more troubling experience—our first brush with piracy.

We were 30 miles from Galle, and less than ten miles offshore, when a large fishing boat came alongside and began asking for food and items of clothing. We offered a couple of

T-shirts, but they weren't satisfied and became increasingly aggressive. They approached closer and closer, until only inches separated us as we continued to sail at full speed in the choppy sea. This intimidation continued for some minutes, and they repeatedly made it clear that they wished to board us. I tried changing course, but they followed us and held their position. Finally, the captain shouted a command to one of his crew, who grabbed a long coiled line and stood against the rail ready to jump onto MOONSHINER's deck. His boss shouted again, but the man with the rope seemed hesitant, uncertain what to do next. Again the captain shouted, and again the man at the rail didn't move. He looked at Fluke, and I wondered if the dog was the reason for his reluctance to come aboard.

At that moment either out of anger or fear, or perhaps a combination of the two, Lot had suddenly had enough. At the top of her voice she let fly with a string of expletives that would have done justice to the crew of a Dutch barge. I don't think they understood a word of what she said, but her obvious defiance gave them cause to pause. Or perhaps Fluke was looking particularly hungry. Whatever the reason, they backed off and decided to leave us alone. We were shaken by the incident, as it was our first encounter with hostility since leaving Hong Kong. Later, in Galle Harbor, we learned from other boats that such attacks were common, and the local authorities were unwilling or unable to do anything to prevent them.

Once on board, the pirates normally strip the victim's boat of any re-saleable items such as radios, TVs, or tape players, and take whatever money or other valuables they can lay their hands on. Before leaving they often damage the boat's engine, so the hapless victim is left without any way to communicate what's happened until he or she is able to sail into port—which gives the robbers ample time to make a getaway.

A couple of days later we were monitoring the ham radio when we heard a singlehanding lady skipper, whom we knew, say that she had just been boarded and robbed. The incident had occurred in almost exactly the same spot where we'd been threatened ourselves. Fortunately they hadn't touched her short-wave radio, and so she was able to report the attack as soon as they left. She assured everyone listening that she was OK, but that in addition to taking money and other valuables they'd put her engine out of action. Several boats in the anchorage immediately offered to go out and tow her in, but she insisted that this wasn't necessary, and she arrived safely a few hours later under sail. She hadn't been physically harmed, but she was understandably badly shaken by the experience.

Sri Lanka

"Could I have my souvenir now?" asked the customs officer. Lot and I looked at each other, puzzled. The man had arrived aboard MOONSHINER soon after we dropped anchor in Galle to check our passports and the ship's documents. He asked the question as soon as he'd completed the paperwork. "My souvenir, could I please have my souvenir?" he repeated. We didn't get it. I guess we were slow on the uptake in those days. "Oh, I think I understand," Lot said finally. "He wants us to give him a memento of his visit." She looked around the cabin and saw a small blue Delftware tile that we'd been given before leaving Hong Kong. Typically Dutch, it depicted a windmill in a pastoral setting with a group of cows. It was the perfect gift—we didn't like it anyway, and the only reason we didn't throw it out was because of nostalgic regard for the friend who'd given it. The official would be able to take it home, and treasure it as testimony to the importance of his job and a reminder of his international friends.

"Please accept this," offered Lot. "It's a picture of my home country, and we'd be very pleased for you to have it." Now it was his turn to look puzzled. "I don't want it," he replied. Well, at least that was clear enough. For the first time he looked embarrassed as he said, "I'd like money. Please give me money." We explained that money was unfortunately in short supply on MOONSHINER, and we definitely couldn't afford to give it away. Eventually, we found a compromise by offering him a polo shirt we'd bought in Thailand. He accepted it grudgingly and left. But at least he accepted it, and didn't insist on receiving cash. Later we would meet other government officials who were more seriously dedicated to fostering the spirit of giving on the part of visiting yachts, particularly in Egypt.

A few days after our arrival we left Fluke in the care of friends on a neighboring boat, and set out to explore the island. After a brief stop in the capital, Colombo, we caught the train to the town of Kandy, the country's cultural center. On the journey Lot struck up a conversation with a woman who was returning home after visiting friends in Colombo. "Do you have anywhere to stay?" she asked. "No," said Lot, "but we'll find something when we arrive." "Oh, you don't have to do that," replied her new friend. "We belong to the Kandy Club, and they have accommodation for members and their guests. If they have a room you must stay there." We thanked her, thinking the offer was made out of politeness and that was the last we'd hear of it. But when her husband met her at the station, she insisted that he drive us to the Club to see if they had any vacancies.

To walk through the door of the Kandy Club was to step back in time. It was a living museum to the country's colonial past, and at any moment we expected to see red-uniformed English officers sitting in a haze of cigar smoke, and hear the voices of plantation owners discussing the latest commodity prices in Manchester or London. Our hosts said there was a room available, but only for one night, and after that they were fully booked. We eagerly took the room, sensing that a stay at the Club would be a unique experience, not to be missed.

We followed a wraith-thin ancient attendant clad in a crumpled white jacket, who shuffled, hunch-backed, wheezing, and agonizingly slowly down the long corridor leading to our room. "He must have been one of the original staff," said Lot in a quiet voice. We declined his courageous offer to carry our bags, for fear it might be his last act on earth—reaching our doorknob unaided was accomplishment enough. Later, we ordered tea in the lounge, and when we saw an ancient waiter limping painfully towards us, the teacups rattling in his shaking tray, we thought our ancient friend had returned. But we were wrong. He was just the same vintage, and probably had similar infirmities due to extreme old age—or perhaps, after 60 years working together, they had developed sympathetic afflictions. We enjoyed our stay at the Club, but we stopped asking for any kind of service for fear of causing a fatal accident.

The following morning we moved to a small bed and breakfast hotel. A few days later Lot's friend from the train and her husband took us on a tour of the nearby countryside. Our first stop was the campus of the University of Kandy, where he worked as the registrar. The university had been closed to students for a long time, due to the violence and political turmoil in the country, and as we walked through the deserted campus he told us a harrowing tale. "My assistant came into my office one morning to ask if I was ready for lunch," he said. "I told him I had some work to finish up, and that he should go ahead. I said I'd join him a few minutes later. As soon as he walked outside he was gunned down, and he died on the steps of the building." "He wasn't the one they were after," interrupted his wife. "He was only the assistant registrar, it was my husband they wanted to shoot." Her husband continued the story: "I always arrive early for work, and the next morning when I got to this fountain," he pointed to an ornamental pool in front of us, "it was surrounded by a row of severed heads. They'd been beheaded in retribution for the killing."

Shortly before we planned to leave the island, we attended a large going-away banquet for the crews of the cruising fleet at anchor in the harbor. I sat next to Vlad, a powerfully built and middle-aged Russian from Vladivostok who was circumnavigating with his wife and two teenage sons. I asked him how long he'd been cruising. He laughed, and replied in excellent English, "For about twenty-five years, it's a great way to see the world." I didn't bother to ask him how he'd managed to get permission from the Soviet authorities to cruise the world at the height of the Cold War. I suspected I didn't need to. His account of many coastal locations in the West left little doubt that he knew them well. A couple of years later, when we were living aboard MOONSHINER in Holland, I got to know the British Military Attaché in The Hague—we were members of the same dinghy sailing club. With Vlad's experience in mind I suggested to him that if Her Majesty's government was looking to recruit and finance an itinerant sailor then Sparham/007 was their man. He didn't seem impressed with the idea. Or perhaps I unwittingly financed his next cruise.

16. The Arabian Sea

A leading reference book for cruising sailors describes conditions in the Arabian Sea at the height of the northeast monsoon as "delightful," with winds averaging between 10 and 15 knots. So we weren't too concerned, for the first couple of days, as we struggled to make progress in zephyrs that averaged only five knots—we were sure that conditions would soon change. But they didn't. Day followed day with hardly a breath of wind. Surrounded by an ocean as smooth as glass and as blue as the cloudless sky overhead, we sheltered from the sun under the cockpit awning, and listened to the beat of the engine. MOON-SHINER carried enough fuel to give her a range under power of 900 miles. The only problem was that this would leave us 1,300 miles short of our destination, so relying exclusively on the engine wasn't an option. Each evening we told ourselves that tomorrow the wind would arrive and things would be different. And each morning we were disappointed.

We were almost 250 miles from Sri Lanka, and 50 miles off the southern tip of India, when a boat appeared as a dot on the horizon, crossing our course at right angles. In areas where piracy is a serious threat I'm always apprehensive when I see a single boat. Vessels in a group usually mean a fishing fleet, and then I feel reassured that the large number of witnesses would deter an act of piracy by an individual boat. Pirate fleets seem to have gone out of fashion, even in Southeast Asia. I watched it carefully, willing it to hold its course. But the thing I feared most happened: it turned and steered straight towards us.

The closer it came the more my concern grew. There was something alien about the boat that convinced me we might be in serious trouble. About 30 feet in length, and built of what appeared to be flat sheets of rotting plywood, it looked as if it wouldn't survive a moderate blow in protected waters let alone rough offshore conditions. Yet it was 50 miles from the coast, and had been heading even further from land before it changed course. As it drew closer I could see a crew of six or seven men standing on deck. What it was doing this far out to sea I couldn't imagine, and I wasn't keen on finding out.

I told Lot to go below and get out of sight, but to leave Fluke on deck. We had learned during our time in Asia that there is a common fear of dogs that has little to do with the animal's size or temperament, but is based on the threat of rabies—a disease endemic to the regions through which we'd been sailing. Also, Fluke was large and of mixed German shepherd extraction, and although I had no illusions that she would be an effective defense if they were determined to board us, I hoped she might act as a deterrent. The boat approached and began making circles around MOONSHINER, at which point my heart began thumping louder than our engine.

For lack of a better alternative I waved and shouted a greeting. In response some waved back, while others began a heated discussion amongst themselves as they continued to circle us. Finally, their leader indicated they wished to come aboard. With a dry mouth I made a joke of it by laughing and saying, "I've nothing on board." Then, I pointed at Fluke as I rubbed my stomach and added, "she's my only food supply." They laughed back, and appeared uncertain what to do next as they continued to motor around us. I knew that the next few seconds would be critical, and nothing else I could say would alter what was about to happen. I remained silent, and as they made the next circle behind MOONSHINER I turned and waved goodbye, as if I was automatically assuming that they were leaving. After that I kept my eyes fixed firmly ahead, reasoning that if I turned around again I would re-establish a psychological connection with them, and encourage their return. With enormous relief I heard the sound of their engine fading in the distance, and by the time I finally did look back they were already half a mile away. Fluke got an extra ration of food that night, and I broke my rule of only one sundowner being permitted while underway.

The wind remained light and our progress slow. To add to our frustrations, a couple of days after our encounter with the plywood boat, our alternator broke down. Our solar panels gave sufficient power to keep the radio, lights, and instruments working but not enough to keep using the autopilot. Hand steering may be enjoyable on a short spin with friends on a Sunday afternoon, but when sailing offshore some sort of self-steering is almost essential for a shorthanded crew. For the next 12 days we were forced to hand-steer MOONSHINER in three-hour watches, 24 hours a day. After 16 days at sea we were still over 700 miles from Aden, so we decided to change our plans and make an intermediate stop at the port of Reysut in the Kingdom of Oman, about two days' sail away.

The prospect of reaching land in the near future had already raised our spirits, but a few hours after changing course we were treated to the most spectacular display by dolphins we've ever seen. And not by a normal school of ten to twenty animals, but by hundreds—we gave up any attempt to count them. They exploded vertically out of the water and into the air, where they performed great arcing somersaults, their sleek bodies glistening in the sun before crashing down into the turquoise sea in a deluge of spray. Time and again, one after the other, the magnificent animals leapt clear of the water and the display continued without a pause for over half an hour. Then, as if to entertain us with a final *pièce de résistance,* some of them defied gravity altogether by performing tail walks past the boat, holding their entire bodies vertically above the water, with just their tails beating the surface for support. It was a magnificent spectacle, and if I hadn't seen it I wouldn't have believed it was possible.

Oman

Eighteen long days and 1,700 miles after leaving Sri Lanka, we finally dropped anchor, with a sigh of relief, in the Omani port of Reysut on the southern coast of the Arabian Peninsula. One glance told us we'd arrived in a different world. Gone was the lush vegetation of a tropical anchorage. Instead, we looked out over a stark and arid landscape from a man-made harbor as bleak and featureless as its surroundings. It must have cost millions of dollars to construct, but during our week-long stay the only vessels that took advantage of its protection were a handful of cruising sailboats en route to the Red Sea, and three or four old wooden dhows. The large commercial facilities remained silent and unused. It was hard to imagine a harsher environment, and yet what we remember most about our brief stay in Oman is the friendliness of its people.

Since leaving Sabah we had always followed the advice of the cruising couple who had told us not to make an issue of Fluke when checking into a new country. We never tried to hide her when immigration officials came aboard—which, given her size, would have been impossible anyway—but we never made any reference to her either. Not one official had ever raised the question of Fluke's presence; it was as if they all chose not to see her. But despite our past success with this strategy we were concerned about the reception she would receive in the Muslim countries of the Middle East. We needn't have worried.

Shortly after we dropped anchor in Reysut Harbor, a boat arrived alongside containing no less than six officials, resplendent in flowing robes. We sent Fluke on deck while our visitors somehow managed to cram into MOONSHINER's small cabin in order to inspect the boat and complete the necessary paperwork. No mention was made of her until 45 minutes later when, with the formalities completed, the last member of the group was climbing back into their boat. He turned, looked back at Fluke and with a broad smile said "Nice dog" . . . and then they were gone.

The next morning we set out to visit the nearest town,

Salalah. We walked through the harbor enclosure and out onto the road. "I guess we might as well start walking," I said to Lot. After a couple of minutes a four-wheel drive truck, the first vehicle we'd seen on the road, pulled up alongside. "Do you want a ride?" asked the driver in good English. He didn't need to ask twice, and we gratefully jumped aboard. After inquiring where we were from, he asked Lot what she was hoping to see while she was in his country. "Oh, a camel," she said. "I've never seen a camel except in a zoo." "You've never seen a camel," he said, amazed. "We have lots of camels here." He laughed, swung the vehicle off the road, and we bumped our way for the next five minutes across rough open countryside until, to Lot's delight, we came to a large group of the ungainly beasts. He stopped for a few minutes while we admired them, before heading back to the main road and into town. In the next few days we discovered that this type of hospitality was the rule rather than an exception. It was physically impossible to walk more than a few hundred yards past the harbor entrance before someone would stop and offer a lift. Usually it was the first vehicle to come by.

Dua Saudara

One of the most interesting cruising boats in the harbor was a large sloop that had been built in Indonesia by two young German brothers out of ironwood, one of the heaviest and hardest woods in the world. They named her *Dua Saudara* (two brothers), and after gathering together a crew of young backpackers they set out to explore the world. They left with more enthusiasm than experience, and their early adventures were not without problems. First they were dismasted in a gale, and later they broke their propeller shaft, which was of far too small a diameter for the size of boat and engine. They'd spent a year in Goa, on the west coast of India, making repairs before heading west towards the Red Sea.

Over time, individual crewmembers left the boat and new ones arrived to replace them, but essentially *Dua Saudara* remained a small community of adventurous young people eager to explore the world in a unique fashion. One of the brothers and his wife had just had a new baby, who seemed to have no trouble taking to a life afloat. Below deck the conditions were spartan; the interior of the boat was essentially unfinished, and the crew slept in hammocks or in sleeping bags on the cabin floor. There was a large upright refrigerator of the kind found in a normal domestic kitchen that didn't seem to have any visible means of support. "What keeps it upright in a gale?" I asked. "Nothing, sometimes it falls over," was the honest reply. But everyone on board seemed healthy, happy, and untroubled by the rough conditions—what did a little discomfort matter when they were living their dream in the company of good friends.

Aden

The light winds we'd experienced since leaving Sri Lanka continued after we left Reysut, bound for Aden. But at least we'd managed to repair our alternator in Oman, and we were no longer slaves to the wheel. During the five-day passage Lot decided to pass the time on night watches by learning to play the harmonica. Fluke immediately offered her opinion as a music critic, and at the first note she began to howl at the night sky at the top of her lungs. Undaunted, Lot ignored Fluke's protests and continued practicing with all the stoic determination of her Dutch forebears. For the next few nights the waters of the Gulf of Aden regularly echoed to the sounds of this unholy cacophony. Fluke eventually learned to tolerate the instrument, but to tell the truth neither she nor the skipper ever became fans.

Aden is a city of over half a million people in an advanced stage of decay. It had once prospered as an important bunkering port on the shipping lanes between Europe and Asia, but 30 years of civil strife had brought the economy to its knees, and signs of poverty were everywhere amongst its war-damaged and dilapidated buildings. It was a city of dust and dirt. Standing on the waterfront, as a monument to the town's decline, was a tall but badly damaged clock tower. Its exterior was pockmarked with shrapnel scars, and its clock was frozen in time—a perpetual reminder of the exact minute when the strafing attack that caused the damage took place during a recent civil war.

Today the country is one of the 25 poorest and least developed nations on earth. But when Zheng He's fleet arrived in 1413 things were very different. Together with Malacca, the city was one of the main seaports on the trading route from the Mediterranean to India and the Far East. A historian traveling with Zheng reported that Aden had over 7,000 well-drilled horsemen and foot soldiers and that "the city was so rich that the women were covered in jewels—gold earrings inlaid with gems, strands of pearls, bracelets, and rings on their fingers and toes."

The two customs officials scrutinized our passports carefully, and then presented us with a list of a dozen rules and regulations that we needed to follow during our stay. The first was a requirement that we wouldn't bring alcohol ashore. This seemed a reasonable and not unexpected request in a Muslim country. As if to emphasize the importance of this particular rule our hosts asked, "Do you have any alcohol?" "No," Lot and I answered in unison, anxious to make it clear that a wine and cheese party on the beach wasn't part of our planned agenda. "We don't have any alcohol at all," we added rather untruthfully.

"Are you sure? Are you certain you don't have any alcohol?" he insisted. I thought of the copious supply of wine and spirits we had stored in our bilge—to fortify our long passage up the Red Sea—and wondered if MOONSHINER was about to be raided by these devout officials in their zeal to rid the town of possible temptation. We reassured them with such enthusiasm that they must have concluded we were charter members of the Temperance League, and well aware of the evils of drink and the depravity of Bacchus. They looked at each other sadly, and shook their heads. "That's a shame," one of them volunteered. "Today is the last day of Ramadan, and we're having a party but we've run out of vodka—the Russian sailors give us vodka but we've already finished it. Are you sure you don't have any vodka?" They looked at us hopefully.

For most people in Yemen the intoxicant of choice isn't alcohol but *qat*, a mildly narcotic leaf that has become one of the country's largest cash crops. It is said to aid concentration and alertness, and a significant percentage of the population walk around with a large wad of qat held in their cheek, which makes them look a little like lopsided squirrels. Lot and I both tried it (but we didn't swallow, as President Clinton would say). It was like trying to chew on a privet hedge, and any pleasurable sensations eluded us.

17. Red Sea Adventures

The Red Sea has a bad reputation. For boats heading north towards the Mediterranean, the wind is reputed to blow furiously and ceaselessly from the wrong direction—from the northwest—and the combination of unfavorable winds, uncharted reefs, and the perception that pirates lurk behind every headland have made the difficulties of the passage part of yachting folklore. To confirm its evil reputation, the ancients named the sea's narrow southern entrance Bab al Mandab, "Gates of Sorrow." The cruising fleet supposedly heaves a collective sigh of relief when they escape from this watery vale of tears into the security of the Mediterranean. We can't speak for other sailors, but our own fears about the journey, and fears we certainly had, turned out to be groundless and the anticipated dragons were all in our minds. We loved the Red Sea.

We left Aden on April 1, April Fools Day—not the most propitious choice of departure dates, but I guess we weren't superstitious. The wind in the Gulf of Aden accelerates as it funnels through Bab al Mandab, where the channel separating the Arabian Peninsula from North Africa is less than 20 miles wide. So we weren't surprised that the 15-knot easterly, which carried us out of Aden, built to over 30 knots as we approached the entrance just before dawn. We passed through the two-mile-wide channel to the east of Perim Island, which lies in the narrowest part of the strait and has a minimum depth of 60 feet. The combination of strong wind and shallow water produced a short steep sea, but it was an exhilarating ride, and we felt like a cork being fired out of a champagne bottle as we flew downwind through the night.

For companionship and security we'd left Aden in company with five other boats, and the day after passing through Bab al Mandab our small flotilla anchored near the ancient city of Mocha (Al Mukha). In the Middle Ages the town was famous as a coffee exporting port, but we were forbidden by the authorities to go ashore, and spent only one night in the anchorage before continuing our downwind sleigh-ride to Great Hanish Island, 35 miles to the northwest. It was still blowing a gale, and MOONSHINER arrived at the uninhabited and starkly beautiful island in less than five hours. One boat left Mocha early, and by the time we approached the island its crew had rowed ashore and climbed a nearby hill to take photographs. They snapped a shot of MOONSHINER, running along the coast at over seven knots under a scrap of foresail and double-reefed main. At almost the same instant we took our own photo of the approaching island from MOONSHINER's deck, and the two images capture the same moment from very different perspectives.

We spent four days at Great Hanish waiting for the southerly wind to drop below gale force. Finally, the wise skipper of an Australian boat said, "We'll be dead from old age before this bloody wind stops blowing. It's taking us in the right direction, so let's go." We all agreed this made sense—and didn't understand why we hadn't thought of it ourselves—so off we set once again on our roller-coaster ride to the north. It was a good decision, because the gale force wind was localized, part of the acceleration effect through Bab al Mandab, and less than 30 miles from the island it lost its venom and by sunset it was down to a moderate 15 knots. Two days after leaving Great Hanish we arrived at Harmil Island in Eritrea, and the southerly wind was replaced by a light five-knot breeze from the northwest.

The Red Sea wind has a fickle personality, and we soon learned to read its moods. Sometimes it would fall light, almost a dead calm, and then we would make haste while it slept, and motorsail towards our next destination. At other times it would awake and roar angrily out of the north with an intensity that denied all hope of progress, and then we stayed put, and relaxed in whatever anchorage we found ourselves until its fury was spent. Sometimes, when it was in a good humor, it would graciously blow a perfect 15 knots and provide a few hours of idyllic sailing. But these moods were rare: it was a wind that enjoyed extremes and preferred to spend its time caressing with faint zephyrs or venting its rage with a full gale. But after Harmil Island, whatever its mood, it always came to visit out of the north.

I'm sure there are worse places than the reef-infested coast of Sudan to have your engine quit, but there can't be many. One morning the flotilla was motorsailing in light winds and a calm sea when our diesel began making noises that would have put Thor and his hammer to shame. We immediately shut it down, and advised the other boats via the VHF radio of our problem. Since leaving Hong Kong I'd learned a lot about engines but I was still no expert, and so I was grateful for any assistance they might be able to offer.

Scott and Gretchen aboard SHADOWFAX arrived first, and they towed us for the remainder of the day until we reached the isolated anchorage at Trinkitat Harbor. Its name is wishful thinking: there is no harbor, just a protected bay surrounded by low-lying land and a fringing reef, and we didn't see a living soul in the place. Once everyone was safely anchored, the other skippers came aboard to lend their collective expertise to solving our problem. After listening to the engine a consensus was reached: "It's either a valve, or you have a cracked cylinder head." Lot exclaimed, "Oh great, so what do we do now?"

It made sense to delay stripping down the engine until we were in a location where there was some possibility of ordering spare parts. But the nearest town of any size—the old slave trading port of Suakin—was over 50 reef-infested miles to the north. "Don't worry, we have more than enough power to tow you all the way if necessary," said Scott. The weather cooperated, and the seas remained glassy calm as we followed the narrow twisting passage inside the reefs, close to shore. We anchored the next night in Marsa Ibrahim, and continued our journey the following day, arriving in Suakin in the early afternoon.

Today, the once important port of Suakin lies in ruins; its fine old coral buildings are in the final stages of collapse. It's sad to see such decay in a town that can trace its history to the time of the ancient Egyptians. For centuries it was the most important African port on the Red Sea. Its fortunes enjoyed a brief resurgence with the opening of the Suez Canal, but the surrounding reefs made the port unsuitable for modern vessels, and in the early 1900s Port Sudan became the country's principal harbor. Suakin went into decline.

Our first priority, after we were securely anchored in the harbor, was to repair our broken engine, and it was a great relief to discover that the cylinder head was intact and only a valve needed replacing. Within a couple of days, with everyone's help, our Yanmar was stripped down, repaired and reassembled, and we were ready to move on. In the process we learned a great deal about how to fix our engine—knowledge which has since proved invaluable. But even more important, we learned to appreciate the willingness of our fellow cruisers to apply their skills and resources in helping one another. Later, we presented each boat with a logo T-shirt to honor their status as members of the Turtle Club Towing Team in memory of the occasion. Scott and Gretchen made the T-shirts, and theirs is another story of ordinary people making their dreams come true.

SHADOWFAX

Scott had worked as a real-estate broker selling island property in Florida, and his wife, Gretchen, had worked as a waitress. "I only took the job because I got to use the company boat," he admitted. Eventually they managed to save enough money to buy SHADOWFAX. She was a large old sloop with a powerful engine, and pilothouse windows large enough to provide an excellent view but swallow half the ocean if they ever broke. But her looks were deceptive, because when we first met Scott and Gretchen in Thailand they had already sailed her halfway around the world.

After buying SHADOWFAX they didn't have much money left to finance their cruise, but they were young and optimistic so they set off anyway. By the time they reached Tahiti, a few months later, they were out of cash. Faced with the possibility of having to sell the boat and give up their dream they urgently needed to earn some money, but how? Back in the States Gretchen's hobby had been making silk-screen prints, and Scott liked to draw, so they put their skills to work. With their few remaining dollars they visited a local store, bought a supply of plain white T-shirts, and then rowed around the anchorage offering the shirts for sale with a picture of each boat printed on the front. It was an instant hit, and although it didn't make them rich it financed the remainder of their five-year circumnavigation. They even sold a couple of hundred to the skippers of diving charter boats—who resold them to their customers as promotional souvenirs—while they were sailing up the Red Sea. They didn't earn a lot of money, but the secret was that their needs were simple: if SHADOWFAX was full of water, fuel, and food, they would happily cross an ocean with twenty dollars in their pocket. Their lifestyle wasn't for everyone, but they had certainly escaped from the cycle where life is defined by the gloom of Monday morning and the relief of Friday afternoon.

Dinner Ashore

In Sudan, visiting sailboats are officially tolerated rather than welcomed. Its Islamist government has been repeatedly accused of supporting international terrorism, and for years it has been conducting a ruthless civil war against its own Christian community. It is a police state and its record on human rights is abysmal. It is also one of the very few countries left in the world where slavery and forced labor are still condoned. Fortunately, the attitude of the country's repressive and xenophobic government didn't prevent many local people from offering us a warm welcome.

"Do you know where we can get drinking water?" Lot asked Hassan the first time he rowed up to MOONSHINER in the anchorage. He was a powerfully built man in his early 30s, with an impressive black beard, and dressed in a spotlessly clean loose-fitting white cotton gallabiya and white turban. "Tell me how much you want and it'll be delivered to the dock tomorrow morning," he replied. He was as good as his word— although it took us a while to realize that the donkey cart loaded with two ancient and rusting 45-gallon fuel containers was our water delivery. When we transferred it to our water tanks we added more water purification tablets than normal, but we suffered no ill effects: the tablets either did their job, or the water was cleaner than we thought.

A few days later Hassan returned with an invitation. "Would you like to eat some traditional Sudanese food?" he asked. "My cousin runs a hotel near the town and he can prepare a good dinner at a good price." Lot answered, "It sounds like fun, but where is it and how do we get there?" "I'll arrange the transport," offered Hassan. "We'll meet on the dock at seven o'clock tomorrow night." "But what about the curfew?" Lot asked. "The police told us we can go ashore but we must be back aboard by six in the evening." "Don't worry, I'll arrange everything, there'll be no problem with the police." said Hassan expansively. Famous last words, I thought prophetically.

Well, cruising yachties are a game bunch, always good for a bit of clandestine adventure, so the next night found twenty of us waiting on the wharf for our transport to arrive. It was pitch dark when two old trucks finally appeared, their headlights ominously turned off. From inside one of the cabs Hassan's voice assured us that these were our limousines. We piled into the back of the two vehicles, and made ourselves as comfortable as possible on the hard wooden planking. Soon, the town was

left far behind as we drove out into the desert, the trucks bang-
ing and crashing their way erratically along the bumpy, winding road. Where we were heading only Allah knew. The thought
occurred to me that perhaps this wasn't such a good idea after
all, and the local slave market was going to be enhanced by 20
ransomable foreigners.

After what seemed like an age, but was probably no more
than half an hour, we arrived safe but sore at our destination.
As the circulation slowly returned to our limbs we looked
around at our new surroundings. We were impressed—the hotel
really did exist. Although what exactly it was doing located in
the middle of nowhere I couldn't imagine. And while it wasn't
in the five-star category, it was clean and tidy in an austere sort
of way. We were met at the door by Hassan's relative. "Welcome, follow me. We've arranged tables in the garden." As we
filed behind him through the entrance, a small group of locals
who were talking, smoking, and drinking coffee in the lobby
fell silent as we passed and eyed us with disapproval.

A dozen candle-lit tables had been set up on the grass—the
first *green* grass we'd seen since leaving Sri Lanka. And the garden had been illuminated with long strings of colored lights,
making an attractive setting for the meal. Soon the food started
to arrive, and it was everything that Hassan had promised and
more. It was excellent. The small hotel had made every effort to
ensure that the evening would be a success, and it looked as if
they had succeeded. Everyone relaxed and began noisily enjoying the food.

We had just finished the appetizers when Hassan returned
in a state of great agitation. "So sorry, but you all have to leave.
You must all leave in five minutes." This didn't go down at all
well with the assembled party, who were just getting into the
swing of things: "No way, I'm not leaving 'till I'm finished." . . .
"Who says we have to go?" . . . "That's crazy. Why do we have
to go anywhere?" were a few of the predictable responses. Hassan's agitation visibly increased. "I'm sorry but you don't understand. You must all leave—it's important to leave as soon as
possible." Just at that moment the kitchen staff, unaware of

whatever problem had developed, arrived with the next course, and a compromise of sorts was reached: we could eat whatever was on the table, providing we did it as fast as possible. We didn't know what the consequences would be if we delayed, but we were all well aware that this wasn't a country where you told your children to ask policemen for directions. So within ten minutes we were climbing back into the trucks for the return trip to the harbor.

We never discovered what prompted the sudden change of heart, and Hassan wasn't willing to talk about it. A table had been set up in the garden for some of the officials whose approval Hassan had required before the dinner could take place, and at least two of these guests appeared to be policemen of some sort. Amongst the yachties it was rumored that he must have accidentally missed an important name off his invitation list, and that this unwitting slight had prompted our early exit. On the other hand one of the younger women in our group had been not been conservatively dressed by strict Muslim standards, and this may have given cause for offense. We may not have had time to enjoy our meal, but the evening didn't lack excitement.

TETHYS

Another boat in our Red Sea flotilla was TETHYS, a sloop from Seattle that was being sailed around the world by her competent two-woman crew under the command of her skipper, Nancy. We had first met them in Ao Chalong, Thailand, and had been following much the same route across the Indian Ocean and into the Red Sea ever since. On the night of our wild ride through Bab al Mandab, TETHYS had been a couple of miles ahead of us when she tore her mainsail as she was passing Perim Island. Not wanting to enter the Red Sea without a fully functioning main, the women dropped the sail, brought their sewing machine into the cockpit, and proceeded to repair it while roaring downwind under their foresail in the pitch-black gale. Now that's what I call discipline.

Understandably, for a woman who was leading a female crew on a voyage around the world, Nancy was shocked by the restraints imposed on Muslim womenfolk. So when she saw a group of local Suakin women chatting on the dock she decided to strike a blow for women's liberation by inviting them for a ride in her dinghy. To their credit, three of them accepted Nancy's invitation, and laughing and giggling they slowly circled the anchored sailboats with Nancy at the helm. They were an attractive if unusual sight: like most African Muslim women they wore the colorful traditional *toup*, a shawl made of thin cotton or silk that is draped loosely over the head and body.

When Nancy returned her passengers safely to the dock, she found that a queue had developed. Lot jumped in MOON-SHINER's dinghy, and soon she was helping Nancy meet the demand for joy-trips around the harbor. All went well until a couple of men showed up, presumably disgruntled husbands. We didn't speak a word of the language but we had no trouble understanding that they didn't exactly approve of their women's behavior. With a few backward looks of regret towards the harbor, the women were soon shepherded away. I fear that Nancy will have to wait a long time before a hypothetical Suakin Yacht Club admits women members, even in purdah.

Several years later, back in Seattle, Nancy raised the funds to purchase TETHYS and now she makes a living teaching sailing to women who sign on for major offshore passages.

The day before our planned departure, we visited various government offices to get our exit papers stamped. "You must leave within 24 hours," we were warned by one of the cold-eyed customs officials as he handed back our documents.

We awoke the next day to the sound of the wind howling in the rigging. Needless to say it was blowing out of the northwest, which meant we'd have a devil of a time making any progress. The situation was serious, as it was essential we reach the next anchorage before nightfall in order to stay clear of the reefs. We were reluctantly in the final stages of preparation,

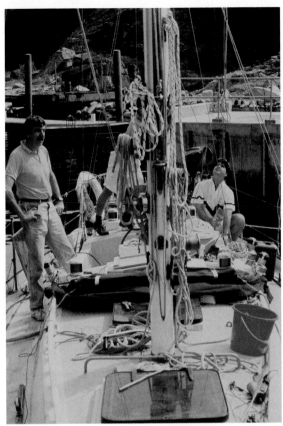

Preparing for
the voyage
(Hong Kong)

oonshiner's first landfall in the Philippines (Puerto Galera)

Taking a shower
(Malampaya Sound, Philippines)

Rey on Mount Capoas (Malampaya Sound, Philippines)

t and Fluke at the mouth of the Kuching River (Sarawak, Borneo)

uke leaving Singapore

At anchor in Malacca Strait (Malaysia)

Ao Chalong (Phuket, Thailand)

onshiner approaching Great Hanish Island (Red Sea)

*roaching Great Hanish Island, as seen from onboard *Moonshiner*
*h pictures were taken at the same time)

Lot's trophy—fishing off the coast of Sudan (Red Sea)

The flotilla at anchor off the coast of Sudan (Red Sea)

ding upriver (France)

kdown on the Meuse River (Joigny-sur-Meuse, France)

Strong trade winds in mid-Atlantic

Grenadine anchorage (Caribbean)

when I saw a boat approaching with the harbormaster onboard. "You can't leave today . . . too much wind. Very dangerous if you leave now. Spend another day and wait until the weather is better," he shouted. "But our papers are no good after today," I said. He replied with a smile, "Not a problem, you can stay as long as the weather is bad, you mustn't go out now . . . too dangerous." He soon convinced us that his offer was genuine, and we gratefully accepted his suggestion. Later that day he came back and presented us with a gift of some fresh bread.

18. North into Egypt

For the next couple of weeks our flotilla made its way slowly up the Sudanese coast. Each afternoon we anchored in the narrow protected channels known as marsas, making sure we arrived while the sun was still high enough for us to see the reefs. Two of the skippers were enthusiastic windsurfers, and as soon as they were safely at anchor out came the boards. As MOON-SHINER was the slowest boat in the fleet we were invariably the last to arrive, and the sight of their gossamer-like sails dancing across the whitecaps conveniently marked the entrance to many obscure anchorages. In the evenings after dinner, Jeff on INTER-MISSION would sometimes relax in his cockpit by playing the saxophone—not exactly a common sound by the shores of the Nubian Desert.

It was just after dawn, the sun barely above the horizon, when we began following the narrow twisting channel out of an overnight anchorage. The only navigational aids were infrequent crude markers, little more than sticks attached to the coral to mark the edge of the passage. Suddenly, Lot cried out in alarm "Look out, you're about to hit the reef." Before I could react I heard a muffled scraping noise as the side of the hull ground slowly along the coral heads. We knew we were taking a chance in leaving earlier than usual, before the sun was high enough to properly see the coral, but we had a long passage to make that day before it became too dark to find the next anchorage. When we later dove under the boat to check for damage, the only evidence of our encounter was a long scratch in the bottom paint. Once again, we had reason to be thankful that MOONSHINER was built out of steel.

We saw few signs of habitation, but camels were often visible through binoculars, and no matter how isolated the anchorage, within an hour of our arrival an armed guard would arrive to check us over. They would appear quietly and on foot, and then take up a position on the nearest piece of high ground and simply keep us all under observation until we left the next morning. We assumed that they were army, but they never approached close enough to be sure.

Fish and Food

Anyone looking at the barren Sudanese coastline might wonder how anything, even a camel, could survive for long in such a harsh environment. But beneath the water of the Red Sea it's a different world—a world that is lush, rich, and pulsating with life. The coral is everywhere ablaze with color, and the Red Sea has long been recognized as one of the world's underwater jewels by diving enthusiasts.

The small fish that inhabit the coral reefs are a food source for their larger cousins, and it's ironic than in a country where tens of thousands live on the brink of starvation we caught more fish off the coast of Sudan than anywhere else in the world. We had a daily competition between the boats in the flotilla to see who could catch the greatest volume of fish in a fixed amount of time. We laid out the fish nose to tail on the deck, and the winner was the vessel with the longest row. Initially, the time limit was two hours, but as the winner accumulated over 50 feet of fish, the duration of future tournaments was drastically reduced. For a lure we used a single hook dressed with thin strips of rubber cut from party balloons, and we trolled at whatever speed we happened to be sailing. They skipped along the surface as we made no attempt to weight the lines, and the tuna seemed to find them irresistible. A fish often jumped onto the hook before we had time to let the line all the way out, and in less than 15 minutes we usually caught far more than we could possibly eat. But nothing went to waste; any leftovers were dried in the rigging, and then turned into fish-jerky for Fluke.

Marsa Halaib

We had been warned that the border between Sudan and Egypt was an area to be avoided. Several yachts had recently been fired on, and then robbed by official-looking craft with deck-mounted guns and crews, in military uniform, who bristled with automatic weapons. We were well aware that in Sudan, as in other parts of the world, the authorities often *are* the pirates. As we approached the border the situation was especially volatile, as an assassination attempt had recently been made on the life of the Egyptian president, Hosni Mubarak.

At the southern end of this dangerous region lies a well protected anchorage that sits in a geographical no-man's-land; our charts indicated that it lay 18 miles to the north of the political boundary between Sudan and Egypt, and 80 miles south of the administrative boundary. The area in between seems to be ruled by whoever has the most firepower—rather like the old Wild West. We planned to make this our last anchorage in Sudan, before heading well offshore until we were safely inside Egyptian territory.

Approaching the anchorage was like entering the Gulag—complete with barbed wire, armed guards, and watchtowers. The whole area was a military base, and we barely had the anchor down before a boatload of representatives arrived from the nearest barbed-wire enclosure. Six of them came aboard, wearing soiled olive-colored T-shirts, and their leader boasted a ragged chevron that was in the final stages of falling off his shirt. They pointed their automatic weapons in our direction, and sullenly demanded to see our passports. To say they didn't exude friendliness would be an understatement.

I have dual Canadian and British citizenship, which means

I have a choice of what nationality I want to be on any given day. Normally I find that the Canadian passport evokes a friendlier response, particularly in areas like the Sudan where the recollection of British colonial occupation doesn't conjure up nostalgic memories. They took it, passed it around for a few minutes, and finally gave it back without comment. Then it was Lot's turn. Normally her passport evokes even less reaction than mine, but not on this occasion.

"You are from Holland?" asked the leader of the group in French. "Yes, from The Hague," she replied. "Ah! Then you know Ruud Gullit," he said, his face relaxing its austerity a little. "Oh yes, I know him well, he's a great player." He turned to his companions, who presumably didn't speak French, to inform them that the woman *knew* Ruud Gullit, one of the world's leading soccer players and captain of the Dutch national team. They broke into an excited chatter, and nodded towards Lot with such enthusiasm they must have thought she was Gullit's sister. Gone immediately was the hostility and the pointing guns, everything was cordial as they lay down their weapons and sat on the deck asking us what we thought of the different European soccer teams, and their chances of success for the coming season.

"Would you like some tea?" offered Lot. So there we sat, surrounded by barbed wire and guns, having an amiable chat with a group of guests whose appearance would have struck fear into the hearts of the toughest gang members in Southside Chicago. After a while they got up to leave, but not before insisting that they would be delighted to show us around their town. "We're very tired at the moment," Lot explained. "Perhaps tomorrow."

Later that evening we were listening to the news on Voice of America radio. I wasn't paying much attention until I heard the announcer declare that the Egyptian government had identified the origin of the recent assassination attempt on the President: "The Egyptian government announced today that . . . the would-be murderers came from the Sudanese terrorist training camp at Halaib." We looked at each other. I rushed below and grabbed the chart, just to be sure. "Welcome to Marsa Halaib," I said. A few minutes later we heard the sound of approaching helicopters. Two huge machines with twin rotors approached from the north, and after flying briefly over the camp they stationed themselves for a few minutes over the bay, their downdraft causing instant whitecaps on the water, and their Egyptian markings and protruding guns clearly visible. After a few moments they disappeared back towards the north. The incident took place in 1992, when Osama Bin Laden's base of operations was the Sudan. We had planned a brief snorkeling trip for the following morning before our departure. We cancelled it.

Egypt

We crossed into Egyptian waters without any further incident after an overnight passage during which we kept well clear of the coastline. After that we continued to anchor each night in the marsas that were conveniently located at regular intervals along the coast. Marsas are narrow winding indentations that cut into the low-lying foreshore and provide excellent protection against the unpredictable winds. We found fewer off-lying reefs than further south in Sudan, but the scenery was very similar. The coastal mountains rose in the west to over 6,000 feet, and between them and the sea lay a wide, featureless, arid, coastal plain. But in the evening the parched land would be transformed into gold, as we sat motionless at anchor, without a breath of wind to disturb the silence, and watched the slow descent of the hazy sun towards the distant peaks. It was magic.

Towards the end of May we arrived in the large tourist town of Hurghada, where we had to complete the official Egyptian entry formalities. A friend warned us over the ham radio that it was like walking through a minefield of corruption. He cautioned us, "They'll take you at every opportunity, so be sure to use the services of an agent. They'll overcharge you too, but it's still cheaper than trying to get through the process by yourself." We thanked him for his advice. He added, "Oh, and one last thing: beware of the police-pass scam. They'll tell you that you don't need one, but when you try to leave, the story changes."

We spent half a day with our agent, visiting various government offices whose stamps and signatures we required, before he finally announced that we were finished. "What about the police pass?" asked Lot. "We've been told it's very important to get one." "It's not necessary anymore," he replied. Lot retorted, "It was necessary two weeks ago, and if we don't get one now we're going to have problems later." He managed to look genuinely offended that we could doubt him, and he practically had his hand on his heart as he explained: "It's not necessary anymore. There were too many complaints, and it's not necessary anymore." He was an agent who'd been recommended to us as the "least dishonest," so we foolishly accepted what he said.

When it was time to leave Hurghada we returned to the various government offices to obtain our clearance papers. All went well until we heard the half-anticipated question: "Where is your police pass?" We went through the story of how our agent had assured us that it wasn't necessary, but they knew the script—they'd written it. Heavy shaking of heads followed by mutterings that: "This is a serious problem," was the only response to our explanation. They had the upper hand—they were holding our passports. Finally, in a classic good guy versus bad guy sting, one of them said: "Perhaps the problem can be solved. Please come with me." We were led into a large impressive office where, sitting behind a large impressive desk, was a large impressive figure in a smart blue uniform amply decorated with gold braid.

He was charming as he smiled, shook hands, and asked us to "Please sit down," followed by "How can I help you?" He listened politely as we told him the story, and nodded in agreement as we explained that it was all a mistake and we hadn't intentionally violated his country's rules. He oozed understanding, and for a minute I thought he was about to stand up, shake our hands, and wish us bon voyage. He had our passports in front of him, on the desk, as he reached into a drawer and pulled out a couple of forms. "I can help you," he said. "You will have to pay for a police pass now, but a late pass costs more than if you'd paid for it when you arrived." We paid with as much good grace as we could muster, and stood waiting for him to hand us our passports. He looked across at us sadly, as if he really sympathized with our predicament, and was pained to have the raise the matter. "But before you leave you must pay the fine." "What fine?" I inquired, wondering if the expensive comedy was ever going to end. "Of course, the fine for not having the police pass. I'm very sorry." His final statement of regret was made with such apparent sincerity that I was now convinced he'd bought his uniform from an actors guild supply-store, and this was a retirement job after a successful career on Broadway. I brought out my wallet again and this time successfully paid for our passports to be returned.

The Suez Canal

The Suez Canal lies just less than 200 miles north of Hurghada, and we arrived at the entrance in the first week of June—ten weeks after passing through Bab al Mandab. "Can I have my present now?" asked our pilot. Since coming aboard, less than an hour earlier, he had sat in the cockpit giving the occasional command while systematically working his way through the large plate of sandwiches we'd provided. I replied, "No, not yet, at the end of the day when you leave." He shrugged and kept eating.

Suez pilots always demand a present from transiting yachts. Normally they're looking for around $10 or $20—not a lot of money, and probably less than you'd offer anyway if they'd been a reasonably efficient and friendly companion for the day. But by the time they reach the Suez Canal, most yachts have already endured an obstacle course of graft and petty corruption and everyone anticipates, and resents, this further demand.

We'd been warned to put all our valuables in a safe place and well out of sight, as the pilots considered everything fair game as a souvenir. "It's like having a human octopus on board," as one yachtie succinctly put it after discovering some of her favorite mementos had gone missing.

Our transit of the Canal, to the Fouad Yacht Club in Port Said, took two days, including an overnight stop. To our surprise we liked Port Said, and found many of the people, particularly the staff at the Yacht Club, to be friendly and hospitable. We spent several enjoyable days exploring the city before setting out early one evening for the 230-mile crossing to Cyprus. We were finally in the Mediterranean.

19. The Mediterranean

We had an easy 40-hour crossing to Larnaca. The wind blew gently out of the northwest, and we motorsailed most of the way, arriving early in the morning to find the harbor entrance obscured by a layer of marine fog. We waited for the sun to burn it off, which didn't take long, before heading into the harbor to celebrate our arrival in the Mediterranean. Most of our friends were already there, as we were one of the last boats to leave the Red Sea that season.

We'd scarcely finished tying up to the dock when I heard a familiar voice: "What kept you? We thought you'd never get here." It was Michel from PAX. He and Frances were walking down the dock carrying a large flagon of red wine and grinning from ear to ear. I replied, "Oh well! Didn't you know a gentleman never sails to weather? Isn't it a bit early to get into the wine?" "Frances told me it's your birthday," he said. "Actually, it's tomorrow, but there's nothing wrong with getting an early start." They climbed aboard. "Don't encourage him," said Lot. We'd parted company in Sri Lanka and it was great to see them both again. They'd made much more rapid progress than MOONSHINER, and had arrived in Cyprus three weeks ahead of us. The party was soon in full swing, and I seem to recall that most of my actual birthday was spent recuperating.

Cyprus is a sort of frontier island where two different sailing cultures meet. Many sailors have no wish to wander further afield than the waters of the Mediterranean. They can spend years exploring its beautiful coastline, soaking up the multitude of cultures that the region has to offer, without ever feeling the urge to set out across an ocean. For many of them Cyprus represents an outpost just beyond civilization—a sort of Dodge City on the watery frontier. And like mountaineers who've survived a dash for the summit in bad weather, they count themselves lucky to have arrived in Cyprus intact, and after briefly admiring the view they quickly retreat to their base camps in Greece, Turkey, or Spain.

But for the sailor arriving from the Arabian Peninsula and the Red Sea, Cyprus *is* civilization. It marks the point of reentry into a familiar environment and culture. It's a chance to renew old friendships that were made in Bali, Phuket, or Sri Lanka and plan the next leg of a voyage that will end in London, San Francisco, or Sydney. It's a chance to relax, eat familiar food and drink recognized brands of beer. It's a place to repair the boat, stock up on supplies, take a leisurely deep breath, and enjoy the sense of satisfaction that comes with the knowledge that simply to have arrived is an accomplishment. It's also a place to acclimatize to the financial shock of what the influx of tourists has done to prices throughout the Mediterranean: our days of cheap food and inexpensive fuel were definitely over for a while.

Turkey and Greece

After three weeks in Larnaca we said goodbye to Michel and Frances who left for Northern Cyprus where they had obtained jobs teaching English. And a couple of days later we made an overnight crossing to Turkey and then began a leisurely westward cruise along the coastline of Anatolia, trying to stay clear of the expensive marinas that cater to the summer charter fleet. The high prices are fine if you're enjoying your annual vacation away from the rat race, but they're guaranteed to send the typically impecunious offshore yachtie into early bankruptcy.

Our favorite anchorage in Turkey was at the end of the

Datca peninsula, next to the ancient city of Knidos which was famous as a center of art and culture in the fourth and fifth centuries BC. It has two small adjacent harbors—one facing the Aegean and the other the Mediterranean—and the view from the peninsula of countless islands and headlands glittering in the sun is truly superb. Just above the harbor are the remains of a theatre that 2,500 years ago seated an audience of eight thousand. But the day we visited its only patron was an angry foraging goat that decided I had no right to be in the place. It repeatedly kept butting me until I was forced to concede defeat, and retreated ignominiously to the security of the waterfront. For some reason Lot and Fluke thought this was hilarious, and sided with the goat.

Crete

The port city of Iraklion on the north coast of Crete is a popular destination for cruise ships in the Mediterranean. It is close to the site of the ancient Minoan Palace at Knossos, which was constructed by a Bronze Age culture so old that even for the classical Greeks it had almost slipped into legend. The town is located on the site of the original harbor through which the Minoans spread their culture to the neighboring islands and the coast of Asia Minor 3,500 years ago.

We arrived to find the small and well-protected inner harbor full of local boats. So we joined the other cruising yachts in the outer harbor and tied up, Mediterranean style, to the mile-long breakwater: our bow held with an anchor and our stern secured to the harbor wall. After a few days we grew accustomed to the large cruise liners maneuvering nearby. As they backed out of their slips they sometimes came uncomfortably close to our mooring, but we assumed they knew what they were doing. But one day a large liner came *really* close, and then created havoc by hitting full forward throttle. Most of the neighboring yachts were just tossed around in the wash and sustained little or no damage, but MOONSHINER was directly in line with the white torrent of foaming water that came rushing backwards from the boat's massive propeller.

"My God, we're going under!" screamed Lot. We were literally on our beam-ends, with the spreaders only a few feet above the water—knocked flat by the immense power of the raging wash that was pushing against the keel. Logic said that the more we heeled, the less resistance the keel would offer to the current of water, and so we weren't going to turn turtle. But logic isn't easy to apply when you are hanging on for dear life with one hand and trying to grab the dog with the other. I was also afraid that the anchor would drag and we would be slammed against the harbor wall only a few feet away. I watched, mesmerized, as our bar-taut anchor chain jumped off its roller and cut its way through the steel pulpit and two stainless-steel stanchions as easily as a knife through butter. A few more seconds and the anchor chain would have been sawing at the mast itself. Fortunately, as soon as the ship began to move forward it altered course and the pressure from its wash began to ease.

We patched up the damage as well as time and our rapidly dwindling financial resources would allow. But it wasn't until we reached Holland, and found jobs, that we were able to pay for proper repairs and stop looking like a war casualty.

Sicily

It took us four days to cross the 350 miles of Mediterranean between Crete and Sicily, and smooth seas and a warm sun made it an enjoyable passage. We made our landfall at the ancient port city of Syracuse, and joined the other boats tied stern-to to the quay. Despite the island's worldwide reputation for violence, as the home of the Mafia, we met with more hospitality and friendliness from the inhabitants of Sicily than almost anywhere else in our travels. We loved the place.

We sailed westward along the island's southern coast, stopping at the small fishing villages along the way, and whenever we went ashore people went out of their way to be helpful. In one harbor, fuel could only be sold to commercial vessels able to show the necessary license. So we loaded a couple of empty containers onto our shopping buggy and went in search of the nearest gas station. We'd only walked a couple of hundred yards when a car stopped to offer us a lift, and then took us directly to the nearest pumps. As we climbed out the driver said: "I'll come back in five minutes to take you back to the harbor." Or at least that's what we thought he'd said, as even Lot (the family linguist) has only a few words of Italian and most of the message was communicated with gestures. But sure enough, a few minutes later he returned to ferry us all, including Fluke and the smelly fuel tanks, back to the boat.

"What for ya wanna find a vetynarian?" The ominous voice, just behind Lot's ear, made her jump. He spoke in a gravelly growl—his accent fresh from Puzo's *The Godfather*. She turned. He was a short stocky man with thick black hair, in his early thirties. "Our dog needs a vaccination," she explained. "I'm trying to find a vet within walking distance, somewhere near the harbor." Lot was standing in the chandlery of a small fishing village. She'd just asked the storekeeper if he knew where she could find a veterinarian, and the man had overheard the conversation. "My brother Vinny . . . he has car . . . you be here at six o'clock and we take you to vetynarian." His accent continued to evoked images of black saloon cars, Chicago speakeasies, and offers that couldn't be refused, but after talking to him for a while Lot decided he was basically friendly and that she trusted him enough to accept his offer. Sure enough, at six o'clock he returned with his brother and after loading Fluke in the car they set off in search of the "vetynarian." An hour later, mission accomplished, they returned to the quay. In the meantime Lot and her escorts had become firm friends.

By the standards of the small Sicilian fishing village in which they lived, Vinny and his brother were wealthy men. Together, they owned one of the largest fishing boats in the harbor, and we later discovered their assets also included several apartments near the waterfront. They credited their financial success to the 15 years they'd spent living in Massachusetts, where they had both worked on fishing boats, and carefully saved their money. Eventually they were able to return to Sicily and buy their own boat, and they had subsequently made enough money to begin investing in local property. They were very proud of Sicily, and took us for car rides into the hills to show us the spectacular scenery. Their hospitality was wonderful, and we were able to return a little of their kindness by inviting them to dinner on MOONSHINER with their wives, who were fascinated to visit "such a little boat that has come such a long way."

We sailed along the Sicilian coast in the company of several yachts we had met in Syracuse. Amongst our new friends was a retired London policeman who, before joining the boys in blue, had spent 16 years in the British Army attached to one of the famous Gurkha regiments that have become legendary icons for toughness and endurance. At 6'5" and around 250 lbs he still looked the part, although he was one of the friendliest people imaginable. I guess when you're that big you can afford to be.

We spent several days in a small harbor waiting for a spell of bad weather to pass. There was only one café on the waterfront, and one of its regular visitors was a neatly dressed man heavily burdened by gold chains around his wrists and neck. When he entered, accompanied by an entourage of followers, there would be a pause in the hum of conversation followed by much nodding of heads and muted mutterings of welcome. In our Hollywood filled imaginations we assumed that he was the local mafioso, and I suspect the assumption wasn't far wrong. He spoke reasonably good English, and for some reason, perhaps because he admired his impressive appearance (and later learned of his military background), he took an instant liking to the ex-London policeman, and through this connection all five yachts visiting the harbor fell into his favor. It wasn't long before drinks started to arrive free of charge whenever the yachties arrived in the café, and offers of free dinners soon followed.

The hospitality extended by our local Don was undoubtedly genuine, and I'm sure he had no ulterior motive beyond the fact that friendship with the foreigners provided him with "face" in the small community. But we all began to get a bit paranoid, half expecting brown paper parcels to be thrust into our hands with whispered requests to "leave them with Luigi in Marseille." So, despite his generosity, we were secretly relieved when conditions improved enough for us to leave. It was now October, and the weather was becoming noticeably less reliable, with frequent periods of strong winds and cool temperatures.

Corsica

In mid-November we crossed the Strait of Bonifacio to Corsica. The weather had now turned bitterly cold, and as MOONSHINER had been equipped for sailing in the tropics we had no heater on board. As a makeshift solution we bought plant-pots, which we inverted as improvised heaters over the burners on the cooking stove, but it wasn't very efficient and the pots kept cracking. "Why don't we buy a some candles?" suggested Lot. "If we light enough of them that should give out lots of heat." But we could only find votive candles—the kind used in church, or to illuminate small shrines. "Well, they're better than nothing," said Lot, as she scooped up handfuls of them and deposited them in front of a storekeeper, who probably concluded we were striving for sainthood. We spread a dozen of them around the cabin, and MOONSHINER was soon cheerfully aglow. We were still cold, but the cabin was definitely much prettier.

We spent two weeks in Calvi, on Corsica's northwest coast, waiting for a break in the continual rain and strong winds so that we could make the short crossing to Toulon, in France. A young Frenchman asked if we would take him along, as Toulon was his hometown, and he wanted to get back to attend a family wedding. Finally, we got a forecast that didn't sound too bad, so we set off just before dusk. Less than ten miles from the harbor we were engulfed in a thunderstorm, the likes of which we hadn't seen since leaving Asia. The wind howled with a vengeance, and our young friend looked anything but happy as MOONSHINER began to pound into the rapidly building seas. "I think it might be a good idea to turn around and wait for a better day," I suggested to Lot. Our passenger nodded his agreement enthusiastically, and we turned back towards the harbor with the cold rain coming down in torrents. It was dark now, and the visibility was so bad that we made our approach by radar: the land was completely obscured until we were less than half a mile from the harbor. The next morning our new friend caught the plane.

As usual, patience paid off, and a couple of days later we tried again—this time under blue skies and with a flat sea. We stopped briefly in Marseille before continuing to Port St. Louis at the mouth of the Rhône River, the starting point of our winter route to northern Europe. As we tied up at the marina, white frost glistened on the dock in the afternoon sunlight—it was November 27. Lot announced, "We've left the tropics behind, and I'm going to get some proper heat aboard this boat." Neither Fluke nor I disagreed, so we spent a week installing a diesel cabin heater. As we made our preparations to leave, neither of us could know that the south of France was about to experience its worst flooding in 75 years, and that MOONSHINER was about to be caught in the middle of it. It would take us all winter to reach Holland, and on more than one occasion we didn't think we'd make it.

20. Danger in the Rivers

High in the Swiss Alps, melt water from the Rhône Glacier begins its 500-mile journey towards the Mediterranean. Fed by melting snows from the surrounding mountains, it follows high Alpine valleys that it helped to carve, and disappears into Lake Geneva, before emerging again to continue its journey into France. At Lyon it is joined by the Saône, its principal tributary, and the now mighty Rhône River dominates the landscape as it rushes through the wine country of southern France on its way to the sea. For centuries its strong and turbulent current discouraged its use for transportation. And although the construction of canals and dams has partially tamed its flow, it remains a difficult and unpredictable river for a small boat to navigate.

Port St. Louis lies at the entrance to the delta where the Rhône empties into the Mediterranean. It is a place to un-step the masts, carry out repairs, and take a break before commencing the long uphill journey, against the current, that leads into the heart of Europe. We spent most of December making our preparations at a small shipyard next to a dock where fishing boats, returning from the Mediterranean, unloaded their catch.

One morning some workers were loading boxes of fish into vans waiting on the quay, when Lot exclaimed: "Oh, that's very nice of them, they've given Fluke a fish." I turned to see Fluke happily walking along the dock with a fish that was so large she was barely able to hold it in her mouth. I briefly wondered why they'd been so generous, but I soon forgot about Fluke as I went back to the problem of unscrewing a frozen turnbuckle.

At least I forgot about her until Lot jumped off the boat and ran down the dock screaming "Fluke, get the !!**!! out of there!" Fluke sheepishly appeared from inside a van—presumably the same one in which she'd found her first booty. We looked around to see if anyone else had caught her in the act, but there was nobody in sight. We tied her up next to the boat and pretended nothing had happened, and Fluke immediately fell asleep with a contented and satisfied look on her face. As far as she was concerned, Port St. Louis was a great place.

The Great Flood

We chose the worst possible year to travel up the Rhône, and if we'd known what lay in store for us we'd have spent the winter snugly tied up to the dock in Port St. Louis, even though our bank balance told us we urgently needed to get back to work. Towards the end of December, heavy rains in the south of France coincided with warm and wet weather in the Alps to create perfect flood conditions. When we set out, just before Christmas, the river had barely begun to rise, but the locals warned us that the water was flowing much faster than normal, and that we should be careful. For the first few miles it wasn't too bad. The current averaged three to four knots in mid-channel, and slightly less near the shore. But as MOONSHINER's maximum speed under power was barely six knots, our progress upstream was painfully slow. And yet this was only the beginning; the river was only teasing us, still waiting to show us its real power. The Rhône valley was about to experience its most devastating flood in living memory.

We set off with our two masts lashed on deck in strong wooden supports, and covered with large tarpaulins to shelter us from the heavy rain. We hugged the shore, where the current was weakest, and slowly crawled upstream. As we got close to the town of Arles the flow became noticeably stronger, and in some places we were barely able to make any way against it. But we persisted, and eventually reached the security of the municipal quay near the center of town.

We spent three days in Arles—a lovely and picturesque town famous for its Roman ruins, and as the home of Van Gogh during some of the painter's most prolific years. The only things we didn't enjoy during our visit were the weather, which remained wet and blustery, and the fact that the river gave no sign of slowing down. I said to Lot, "We might as well push on, or we could be here all winter. We'll carry on hugging the river-bank and try to take it easy on the engine." So once again we launched ourselves into the turbulent Rhône, and struggled up-stream towards our next destination—the city of Avignon.

After a couple of miles the river narrowed, and the current increased to over five knots. We'd already discovered that the speed of the water varied, depending on the river's width, depth, and the influence of curves and bends. So we cranked up the engine as far as the throttle would go, reasoning that we were in a particularly bad spot and if we could only get a few hundred yards further along, conditions might improve. We measured our progress against a navigation marker anchored a few hundred yards ahead, and by continually experimenting with our course we were able to claw our way slowly forward. Our GPS told us that we were traveling at less than half a knot, but the river ahead looked wider. "Another hundred yards, and we'll be past the worst of it," I shouted to Lot above the roar of the hammering engine. There was something truly dangerous and sinister about the power of that formidable current, and the grey gloom of the overcast sky and the pouring rain weren't adding to our confidence.

A loud bang from the engine room shook the whole boat, and the cabin immediately began to fill with smoke. I throttled back the engine, which was making such a terrible noise I thought it must be tearing itself apart. It was still running on one of its two cylinders, but it seemed inevitable that within a matter of seconds we would lose it altogether. Without an en-gine, only our anchor would stand between us and disaster, and if it failed to take hold on the river bottom we would be swept helplessly downstream. Our sails were stowed away in lockers, and our masts were lying impotently on the deck. With less than half our normal horsepower I could still steer the boat, but we were being swept backward at about four knots in the six-knot current.

My mouth was so dry it felt as if I'd swallowed all the sand in the Kalahari. I looked over my shoulder, searching for a possible refuge down stream—somewhere to tie up. Lot said, "I can see something. It looks like a commercial dock. It's Christmas Eve and I don't think anyone would mind if we tied up there." "Right now I couldn't care less if they mind or not," I replied. I angled the bow across the river, to get closer to the bank, as we continued to be swept backward at an alarming rate. "We'll only have one try at this," I warned Lot. "If we can get close enough, and drop the anchor just upstream of the dock, then we should be able to use the current to steer ourselves into the shore, providing the anchor holds." Our timing would have to be perfect, and I wasn't sure the engine would keep running—I didn't know what damage we were doing to it, but I sure wasn't about to turn it off.

Lot stood on the foredeck ready to release the anchor, and I kept my eyes on the rapidly approaching dock, trying to judge our position. I said, "When I tell you to let it go, keep well clear of the chain. If you get caught up in it there's nothing I can do to take the pressure off." We were almost there, but smoke was now pouring out of the cabin. "NOW!" I screamed over the din of the engine. With a splash, the 60 lb. anchor hit the water, followed by 250 feet of chain. It had to hold, or we were in deep trouble. MOONSHINER's backward career came to an abrupt halt, and as I turned the wheel we sideslipped safely into the dock. Lot jumped ashore and secured the lines. "Hey, not bad," I said. "A bit further back than I'd planned, but definitely not bad." My heart was pounding. "Time for a Christmas drink," said Lot. I was already on my way to get the bottle.

We looked around at our new surroundings. We had tied up at the *Halte Fluviale* on the outskirts of Arles—a commercial dock used by small seagoing freighters and large riverboats. It was three in the afternoon on Christmas Eve, and not surprisingly the place was deserted; there was nobody in sight, and we were the only boat. While Lot went in search of someone in authority to explain what had happened, I took a look at the engine. The problem wasn't hard to find. When it had been rebuilt in Hong Kong, someone had failed to properly install a fuel injector as fresh paint had fouled the screw threads. When I ran it at full throttle, the high pressure had blown the injector clean out of the engine block. With a half-inch hole in the top of the cylinder head, it wasn't surprising the engine had made such a racket and filled the cabin with smoke.

Lot returned a few moments later with a new friend. Monsieur Aupy was the General Manager of the Halte Fluviale, and she had found him in his office in the final stages of locking up for the holidays. He assured us that there would be no problem in staying until the engine was repaired, and the river slowed down. But a freighter was due to arrive in a few days, and we would have to move to the end of the dock. "Don't worry about it," he said. "I'll get some men to help you, and we can retrieve your anchor with one of the dock cranes." "Do you know a good mechanic?" Lot asked. "I'll see what I can do," he said, smiling. "Enjoy your Christmas."

The next morning we were leaving the deserted port to take a walk in the town, when Monsieur Aupy drove in through the gates. He had left his family's Christmas celebration to come out and check that we were OK, and that we had everything we needed. Two days later he returned with half a dozen men to help move the boat. The crane operator retrieved our anchor using a dredging attachment, and when it was hauled out of the water it looked like a toy trinket dangling from the hand of a giant. Moving the boat along the dock was easy, as we let the force of the river do the work—the manpower was only needed to slow the boat down, and prevent the Rhône from taking MOONSHINER back to the Mediterranean. A couple of hours later a mechanic arrived, and spent about an hour re-fitting the injector. "How much do we owe you?" we asked when he had finished. "There is no charge. You have come a long way, and it is my pleasure to assist." My opinion of France, and the friendliness of its people, was hitting an all-time high.

We spent a week at Halte Fluviale waiting for the river to slow. During that time a small freighter of about 5,000 tons arrived, and docked skillfully a few yards in front of us. One of the crew told us they had come from Egypt, and their voyage across the Mediterranean was one of the worst he could remember. Battered by gale force winds, their rudder had been damaged, and they were forced to delay their departure from Arles while they made repairs.

Finally we were ready to leave, and after much giving of thanks to Monsieur Aupy and his men, we cast off once again. We figured the current had slowed down just enough for us to make some progress—it was flowing at about four knots—but we were jinxed. Less than ten minutes later, just as we were approaching the marker we had struggled so hard to pass the week before, the engine again lost all power in one cylinder. Lot and I looked at each other with a mix of horror and disbelief as we were swept downstream in a repeat performance of our misfortune a week earlier. "We did it once, so we can do it again," I shouted to Lot. We did. And once more we arrived at Halte Fluviale traveling backwards.

The now familiar face of the mechanic leaned over the engine. "I'm sure it's just something blocking the fuel line, give me a small pair of tweezers and I'll show you how to fix it if it happens again." He disconnected the fuel line and sure enough— there was a large chunk of gook that he quickly extracted. We bled the line, paid the minimal $20 he charged for the visit, thanked him and set off again.

Rescue

Our trip to the ancient town of Avignon was slow but without incident. By the time we reached the municipal marina things were looking up; the current had slowed to about three knots, thanks to a few days of sunshine and drier weather. The location of the marina was ideal. Sitting in the cockpit we looked up at the white cliffs beneath the ancient Papal Palace—which had been home to six successive Popes in the fourteenth century. And a couple of hundred yards astern the arched remains of the beautiful twelfth century Pont d'Avignon jutted defiantly into the river. For centuries it had been the only bridge over the Rhône between the Mediterranean and the city of Lyon, 300 miles to the north. But in the late Middle Ages, the cost of repairing the damage caused by frequent violent flooding became so great that the bridge was allowed to fall into disrepair. At the time, we didn't know the reason for its demise; if we had, we might have been less nonchalant as we relaxed on deck admiring the view.

The day after our arrival the rain returned with a vengeance. It began in the late evening while we were attending a concert ashore, and it fell in torrents throughout the night. Just before dawn MOONSHINER started to shudder with a strange resonance, and when I started to hear loud bangs, as flotsam collided with the hull, it was definitely time to go on deck and investigate. I wish I hadn't. The river was in full flood, roaring past the boat at what I judged to be about ten knots. We were tied up on the outermost float—where the current was strongest—and our mooring lines were tighter than the violin strings that had entertained us only a few hours earlier.

The downpour continued throughout the day and the speed of the river increased. We watched helplessly as enormous logs and small trees swept past MOONSHINER, and frequently a large piece of flotsam would catch her a glancing blow on the bow, and the noise of the collision would resonate through the cabin. "We'll be all right, just as long as the dock holds together." I said to Lot. We spent most of our time checking the lines and listening to weather forecasts. Sometime in the mid-afternoon we realized it was no longer possible to get ashore; the road alongside the marina was submerged under the racing water. We were marooned. We looked nervously at the pilings that supported the floats—if the river rose just three more feet they too would be under water, and then the whole marina would be carried downstream before crashing into the famous bridge astern.

Just before dark, a woman appeared in the cockpit of a nearby boat holding a baby. She was crying, terrified. Her husband had left for work that morning and he was unable to get back to the boat. Apart from the child she was alone. Lot tried to reassure her, and together we listened to the rain and watched the river's inexorable rise as night fell. Just before midnight we heard a shout of alarm, and shot out of the cabin to see what was wrong. A few yards away the upstream float, which was bearing the full force of the current along its whole length, had capsized and turned upside down. From one end to the other it was bent into an arc by the force of the water, and I was sure it was only a matter of minutes before it broke up completely. If it did, the remnants, together with the half dozen large boats attached to it, would come crashing down onto the rest of the floats like a battering ram. The whole of the marina was in serious danger of being swept away if that happened.

Everyone in the marina was awake and dressed, wondering what would happen next. Before long we heard the sound of outboard engines, and a few seconds later the fire department arrived in inflatable dinghies and began the slow process of evacuating everyone. "It's kind of ironic, that after ten thousand miles of ocean sailing we're about to be rescued by a fire brigade on a river in the south of France," observed Lot. But rescued we were, along with everyone else, and I must admit it was a huge relief to be safely back on dry land.

Later that morning, when the rain stopped and the sun began breaking through the clouds, we climbed to a high point at the top of the cliffs near the Papal Palace. We looked down onto the marina, where MOONSHINER was proudly stemming the flood; she was the furthest boat from the shore and the most exposed. From our vantage point we could also see what was supporting the capsized float: someone must have left their boat in the marina for the winter, and had lashed its 60-foot mast securely to the dock. It was this mast, bent like a drawn bow, which was holding the whole structure together.

The response of the marina operators to these events was a public relations tour de force. The morning of our rescue the marina manager invited all the evacuees to a meeting. "On behalf of the city of Avignon I apologize for what's happened." he began. "We can't be responsible for the weather, but you all had the right to expect a safe place to tie up your boats and so the city would like to pay your expenses to stay in a hotel until its safe for you to return. We will pay for a two-star hotel, but you can make up the difference for a more expensive hotel if you wish." We found a small comfortable hotel near the marina, and were it not for my concern for MOONSHINER, I would have been happy to see it rain for the rest of the winter. Within a couple of days the river had fallen far enough for us to return to our boats, but it was almost six weeks before the current was slow enough for us to continue our journey.

Headlines in the papers and on the TV throughout Europe announced that this was the worst flooding the region had seen in almost 100 years. Helicopter rescues had saved many lives in areas where the river had broken its banks, and the flood was a disaster affecting the whole of south-central France. We certainly didn't enjoy the experience, but if you must be stranded somewhere, it would be hard to find a more pleasant location with more hospitable hosts than the city of Avignon.

21. Fame in the Canals

By the third week of February the river had slowed down enough for us to continue our journey. But it was still running faster than normal, and it took nine days for MOON-SHINER to cover the 150 miles from Avignon to Lyon. The last couple of days were a difficult struggle in heavy rain and a rising current that we feared might herald the onset of a new round of flooding. We spent a week in the city waiting for the weather to improve, before tackling the Rhône's major tributary, the Saône.

In good summer weather the Saône would be delightful. We followed the river through a lovely landscape of rolling hills and broad valleys, and tied up each night to the riverbank in protected backwaters or at the quay in one of the many attractive towns and villages along our route. Town quays were usually free of charge, and conveniently located within walking distance of shops and the local *cave*—where we could take our empty bottles to replenish our wine supply at unbelievably low prices.

But despite the charm of the villages the fact remained that it was still mid-winter, and the cold wet weather remained an ongoing problem. The speed of the current varied daily—depending on the rainfall over the previous twenty-four hours. But it was often fast, and our progress was depressingly slow. We sat in the cockpit for hours, watching the banks of the river crawl slowly past as the rain poured off the tarpaulins and dripped down our necks. Even the cows in the fields looked depressed. We saw very little commercial traffic, and the few pleasure boats crazy enough to be out at that time of year were all, sensibly, heading in the opposite direction.

Finally, we reached the intersection of the Saône with the canal that joins it to the River Marne—the *Canal de la Marne à la Saône*. When planning our route we'd considered following this canal, but had been put off by the prospect of transiting several hundred locks and decided the river was a better option. Lot, who had been sitting silently for some time, finally said, "You know, it's taken us over a week to travel less than 150 miles—that's only 20 miles a day. Are you sure we wouldn't be better off taking the canal?" I thought about it, weighing the odds. It couldn't be any slower than the river— where we were still vulnerable to further flooding—and I didn't relish the risk of a repeat performance of our breakdowns in Arles. "Let's give it a go," I said as I spun the wheel, and headed MOONSHINER towards the entrance lock. "At least we won't get carried downstream if the engine quits. There's no current in the canal."

By the end of the day we had traveled 15 miles and passed through 11 locks. Although our charts indicated there should have been a minimum depth of well over two meters in the canal, we discovered we were unable to reach the bank to tie up, because of heavy silting. So we ran MOONSHINER gently onto the mud, and used a solid plank to bridge the four-foot gap between the boat and the shore. In the morning we backed off the mud using full reverse power, and this became our normal mooring technique in the canals. We usually traveled ten hours a day, and our record distance was 32 miles—which required the transit of 22 locks.

A few days after we entered the canal we went hard aground while trying to avoid a passing barge. A crewman aboard the other boat saw what had happened and threw us a line as they came alongside. I grabbed it, took a turn around one of MOONSHINER's cleats, and waited for the momentum of the passing boat to pull us clear. But the barge was moving faster than I realized, and before I could release the line we were catapulted backwards across the canal. We hit the far bank with enough force to snap the three-quarter-inch hydraulic ram that connects our autopilot to the steering quadrant. Fortunately our rudder still seemed to be OK, but it was a stupid thing to have done and we were lucky to have escaped without more serious damage.

Fifteen Minutes of Celebrity

We left the canal before it reached the Marne as our quickest route to Holland lay down the River Meuse, through the city of Charleville-Mézières in the French Ardennes, and then north towards the Belgian border near the town of Givet. As soon as we entered the river our speed doubled—we were finally heading downstream and the current helped to push us along. Struggling against the flow in the Saône and the Rhône we had averaged less than two knots, but now we were flying past fields and forests at more than eight. Spring was in the air, and leaves began to appear on the trees that shaded the riverbank— where ducks were busily occupied in guarding their chicks. The weather was warmer too, and sunshine began to dry the sodden landscape. The long hard slog from the Mediterranean seemed almost over, and our spirits were high as we anticipated arriving in Holland within a couple of weeks.

Twelve miles downstream from Charleville lies the sleepy rural village of Joigny-sur-Meuse. Here the river twists and turns along a narrow valley as it cuts its way between steep tree-covered hills. Just before the town a small lock, overlooking a picturesque weir, gently lowered MOONSHINER four feet closer to sea level—and her destination. As we prepared to leave, Lot helped the lock keeper to cast off our lines while I got ready to start the engine. Just before the gate opened I turned the key in the ignition. For a fraction of a second the engine turned—and then there was a loud BANG, followed by silence. I knew immediately what had happened and my heart sank. Water had somehow found its way into the engine and the piston had slammed into it. Just when we thought we were home free, we were suddenly in deep mechanical and financial trouble.

Lot, with her fluent French, was the family translator. "Please tell the lockkeeper we've lost our engine," I said, surprised at how calm and reasonable I sounded. "Ask him where we can tie up." After a few moments Lot returned. "He says he'll help to pull us out of the lock, and then we can tie up a few yards downstream where we won't block the entrance."

That afternoon I took the head off the engine to check out the problem. It couldn't have been worse. One of the cylinder liners—the steel "chimney" in which the piston moves up and down—had cracked through the middle and was literally in two pieces. As if that wasn't bad enough, the force of the impact had bent the connecting rod, and when I tried to remove the piston assembly it wouldn't budge. It should have been possible to lift it vertically out of the engine block, but the bent rod meant that the hole wasn't big enough. Whenever I tried, I heard an ominous *clunk* as something got caught up inside the bowels of the engine, and the piston refused to move any further. Thousands of miles after leaving Hong Kong, and less than 150 miles from our destination, we were well and truly stuck.

"I need to get the piston out to see how much damage has been done before we can decide what parts to order," I said to Lot. But how? After thinking long and hard I came up with a solution. The old Yanmar was designed so that owners could do much of their own maintenance. It had inspection ports the size of barn doors, and I discovered they were large enough to actually get my cordless drill inside the engine. If I covered the rod with some sort of dye, I'd be able to see where it was catching when I tried to lift the piston out. So I coated the rod with ink from a felt-tip pen. Now, when I tried to remove the piston, the *clunk* left a telltale mark in the red ink, and I was then able to grind away at the offending spot by working through the inspection ports.

After ten hours of repeatedly re-coating the rod with ink and grinding away at it from both sides of the engine, I finally managed to get the piston out. Now came the problem of finding replacement parts. Lot spent half an hour on the phone to Holland. She returned discouraged: "I must have checked every Yanmar dealer in the country, and nobody seems to know where we can get parts for our model of engine. They suggest we call Hong Kong." We took their advice, and finally ordered the necessary parts through Paul in Aberdeen Marina. A week later we called to check on the status of our order. "They don't have them in stock so it's going to be a few weeks before I can get them out to you," Paul answered. Then came the bad news, "And they're going to cost you three thousand US dollars." "Our financial situation just got a lot worse," I informed Lot.

In Europe most purchases are subject to a VAT, or value added tax, equal to seventeen percent of the purchase price. Except that ships in transit, which MOONSHINER certainly was, were supposed to be exempt. But when Lot visited the tax office in Charleville to get our exemption she was told we would have to pay. "How do we know you're a boat in transit?" asked the surly official behind the counter. He refused to accept the numerous stamped entry or exit papers that we had acquired since leaving Hong Kong as proof that what we said was true. "The only way to verify it would be to send someone out to the boat, and we don't have time to do that—so you'll have to pay." It was an important issue for us, as the tax added hundreds of dollars to the cost of our repairs and we were practically broke. "We'd be happy to pay for a taxi for you to send someone to the boat, it would only take twenty minutes each way," offered Lot. The man was adamant and unmoved. We would have to pay the tax.

It would be hard to imagine a less likely place for a Hong Kong boat to find temporary fame than a rural backwater in northeast France, but that's what happened. Everyday the local postman cycled past MOONSHINER on his way to deliver mail to the lock keeper, who must have told him the story of our journey from Hong Kong and how we came to be sitting for so long next to his front door. One evening the postman was sitting in the village bar enjoying a beer with his friend from the village newspaper and passed on the story. The result was a brief account of our story in the next edition, which we hoped everyone would soon forget. But it wasn't to be. It was still early in the year and the lack of anything more interesting to write about brought a journalist from the largest newspaper in Charleville-Mézières knocking on MOONSHINER's hull a few days later asking for an interview. In addition to the story of our travels from Hong Kong with Fluke, he was interested in the lack of help we had experienced at the hands of the local customs officials. We were more than happy to provide him with information—perhaps the paper could bring about a softening of the taxman's heart?

To our surprise, the story ran as a major spread in the weekend edition, complete with photographs of MOONSHINER and her crew. Our fame was now assured! "I don't believe what he's written," screamed Lot, as Fluke quickly left the cabin sensing the beginning of a major eruption. "Here, listen to this: *A tear trickled slowly down Madame Sparham's cheek as she told your reporter how the tax office . . .* I can't read anymore, its too embarrassing. What's he talking about?" I had to sympathize—crying is something I've seen Lot do only once, and it certainly wasn't in front of a reporter. "Oh well, perhaps we'll get a call from the local tax office begging our forgiveness and promising to waive the tax payment after all," I conjectured hopefully.

The paper came out on a Saturday, and the following evening we held a big party aboard MOONSHINER for the friends we'd made during the six weeks we'd been stranded in the village. The cause of our celebration wasn't the newspaper article, but the fact that we'd just received news that our long awaited parts had finally arrived at the airport in Paris. Lot was leaving at five the next morning to pick them up—it made sense for her to be the one to go as my French would have been woefully inadequate if any problems arose with customs.

The next morning I was awakened by the sound of someone pounding on the hull. I looked at my watch, my head throbbing from the excesses of the night before. It was eight o'clock and Lot was long gone. I peered through the cabin curtains to see various trucks from France-4, one of the country's largest TV networks, discharging people and equipment onto the riverbank while in the foreground a beautiful girl was looking enquiringly into MOONSHINER's cockpit. I stuck my groggy head outside. "Sorry to wake you," said the girl in excellent English—her eyes quickly taking in the scene and comprehending my fragile physical state. "We want to make a program about you and your boat. We'd like to interview you." I glanced into the main cabin—it was a disaster. Cigarette butts and half empty beer and wine bottles were scattered around the cabin, and dirty dishes and the remains of chopped vegetables cluttered the sink—all bearing witness to the recent feast and bacchanalian orgy.

"Can you give me a minute?" I asked. "Of course," she replied with a smile to gladden the heart and clear the head. "We have to set up our equipment anyway, please take your time." I looked frantically around for some way to get rid of the mess. I grabbed a sheet from the bed, and back in the main saloon I laid it beside the table and unceremoniously scooped everything on top of it—bottles, food, dishes, ashtrays, butts, were all piled together in a nauseating heap. I rolled it into a ball, and hurried it out of sight before it had time to ooze its contents onto the cabin floor.

The TV crew spent over half a day filming. I was interviewed inside the boat, and then they followed me around the village as I visited various shops and chatted, in my non-existent French, with the locals. The interviewer asked the obvious questions, such as "What do you think of France?" and I was happy to be able to answer that with the single exception of the local tax office, we loved the place and had received nothing but help from the many people we'd met.

The program aired immediately after the six o'clock news the following Friday evening, a prime viewing time in France. I knew I must have said the right things when the tourists began arriving the next day—scores of them. Busloads of schoolchildren arrived to see the "boat from Hong Kong" and a stream of adult visitors came to say hello and offer us gifts of food and supplies, "just in case you're running short." Their generosity was embarrassing. A farmer even arrived on his tractor pulling a trailer loaded with welding equipment because he'd heard, correctly, that since our arrival we had sustained some damage from a passing barge. It had bent some of our stanchions and he spent the afternoon fixing them. There was something about our predicament that seemed to capture people's imagination and the spontaneous demonstration of genuine concern touched our hearts. But the taxman never called.

I set to work to fix the engine. Lot was understandably skeptical of my mechanical abilities—perhaps remembering the incident when I drilled through CALLIOPE's hull while installing the curtain rail. "If it actually runs when you've finished, you can have *Lobster Thermidor*," she promised one day when I was up to my elbows in grease. It took me almost a week, with frequent references to the engine manual, to get all the parts back where they hopefully belonged. Was everything in the right place? Had I connected it all together properly, or was there going to be another mechanical disaster as soon as I attempted to start it? I disengaged the decompression levers and turned the flywheel over by hand. Everything seemed OK. I took a deep breath, made a brief mental offering to the gods, and turned the key. After seven weeks of enforced silence the engine roared into life. We were ecstatic.

The sun was warm as we said goodbye to Joigny and pointed the bow downstream towards the Belgian border. By now the "broken boat from Hong Kong" was famous, and as we passed through the villages many people came out onto their balconies and waved. Stardom was a new experience, and I began to have fun by giving a royal wave in return—using the back of my hand. Lot exclaimed, "My God, we've got to get you out of here, and in a hurry before you're ruined for life."

We never did receive our tax refund before leaving Joigny, but sometimes life has a strange way of evening things out. The year before our journey through France, the country introduced a charge for private boats using the inland waterways. It was expensive, and the bureaucracy for collecting it wasn't yet fully in place, so before leaving Port St. Louis we had been advised to "Ignore it—with a bit of luck nobody will ask you for a receipt and you can always pay later if they do." We took the advice and didn't pay. But as we pulled into the last lock in France, we saw the lockkeeper holding up a piece of paper in the window of his kiosk. He was asking for proof of payment. "Oh well," I sighed, I guess it had to happen sooner or later. Lot took all our documents, plus her wallet, and went over to talk to him. "Aren't you the boat from Hong Kong?" he asked. "I saw you on the television." Lot confirmed that we were. "Did you ever get a break from those tax people?" She explained that they had remained staunchly unmoved by our pleas, despite the fact that under French law we should have been exempt. They chatted for a while longer, until he finally wished her "Au revoir, bon voyage," and closed his window. The dreaded piece of paper was never mentioned again.

Our transit through Belgium was uneventful, and four days after leaving Givet, with the flags of all the countries we had visited fluttering proudly in the breeze and our horn blaring, we tied up at the marina in Maastricht and opened the bottle of champagne we had been saving for the occasion. We had arrived in Holland, which was to be our home for the next three years.

Part Two

Rotterdam to Vancouver

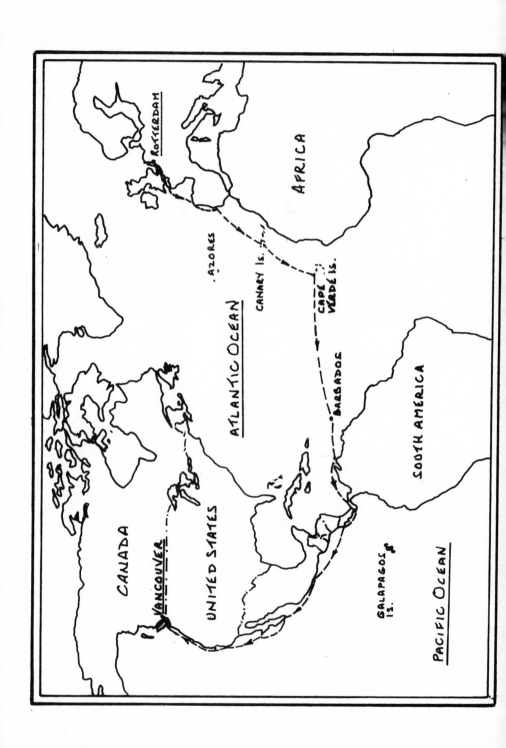

22. Paying the Piper

There are two dimensions to bluewater sailing—two journeys. One has a clear destination and its achievement is celebrated with flying flags and champagne. The other is an inner journey, where we learn about our personal strengths and limitations, and struggle to figure out what we'll do with the rest of our lives when our temporary escape is over. Cruising changes us. And there's no guarantee that the transition back into a *normal* life will be easy. It wasn't for me—freedom can be addictive.

We spent the first couple of weeks in Holland traveling around the country looking for a spot where we could tie up MOONSHINER and continue to live aboard. On a visit to The Hague we ran into an old friend. We sat down for a beer at a sidewalk café opposite the des Indes hotel where I had been staying when I first met Lot. "Are you back in your old haunt?" she asked, pointing across the road. I admitted, "No, I've borrowed my mother-in-law's tent and we're spending a couple of days at a campsite near Scheveningen beach. We're living our life in reverse, and getting poorer as we get older." We all laughed, but the reality stung. My days of traveling first class and staying at five-star hotels were definitely over. We had made our decision to go sailing with our eyes wide open—we knew that losing our financial security was part of the price we must be willing to pay. And payday had arrived.

It had been almost three years since either of us had set an alarm clock for Monday morning, and I wasn't looking forward to resuming the habit. I wasn't looking forward to the prospect of job hunting either, but had no choice—we were basically out of money. But in addition to financial necessity, there was another reason for spending some time in Holland. Lot had lived in Vancouver for six years before my transfer to Hong Kong, but I knew that she had never really felt at home there. She had missed her European friends, her family, and the Dutch lifestyle. Eventually, we were planning to return to Canada and I wanted her to be happy with the decision. I hoped that spending some time in Holland would help.

Holland had changed in our absence. Gertrude Stein said: *"When you get there, there's no there there."* It's one of my favorite quotations as it points to a general truth. It admonishes us to enjoy the day-to-day pleasures of living, and not become too focused on end results. But it also hints of the disappointment that awaits anyone who expects to find people and places unchanged after a long absence. Old friends move on: they develop new interests, grow apart and join different circles. Some marry and have children. Others, who you think are bonded for life, split up or divorce. In this social merry-go-round we lose touch. If we're lucky a few close friendships last a lifetime, but the network of casual relationships that define our daily lives and give us a sense of belonging is constantly changing, even if we never leave home. It had been eleven years since Lot and I first met in Holland, and life had moved on in the meantime. Even The Hague was no longer the familiar place we remembered. Hathor and other favorite hangouts were still there, but the faces inside belonged to strangers.

In Holland, as in many other countries, living aboard your boat is an alternative lifestyle that is increasingly frowned upon. We eventually found a home for MOONSHINER in an ancient marina on the IJssel River, a tributary of the Maas (as the Dutch call the Meuse), 15 miles upstream from the port city of Rotterdam. Lot found a job as Sales and Marketing Manager for a large hotel, and I began circulating my résumé and networked my few remaining contacts in The Hague.

A month later I got a phone call from a tiny consulting company in Amsterdam that had only been in existence for a couple of weeks. A friend had given them my résumé, and as they were planning to make transportation their specialty they were interested in my background in aviation. The president was a part time lecturer at the university in Amsterdam who had previously run the planning department of the now defunct Dutch aircraft manufacturer Fokker. He had good contacts in the government and in industry, and quickly landed us a contract to carry out an airport study in Indonesia.

And so, to my surprise, less than six weeks after MOON-SHINER arrived in Rotterdam I found myself on a plane heading back to Singapore en route to Jakarta. Scarcely twelve hours after leaving Holland the familiar coastline of the Malay Peninsula came into view. The sight rekindled a flood of memories of the two years it had taken us to complete the same journey—under sail—in the opposite direction. From the air, landmarks where MOONSHINER had lingered were clearly visible. But although the view was spectacular, the landscape from 40,000 feet looked sterile and lifeless. The taste of salt spray, the smell of the seashore, the sound of surf breaking on white shell beaches, the sight of seabirds circling over exquisite bays—it all lay far below and far beyond my senses. But I knew those things, that I loved, were still there. And I missed them.

Just before the wheels of the Garuda Airline 747 touched down at Singapore's Changi airport, I looked down on the exact spot where we had spent so many weeks at anchor off the north coast of the island. I suddenly felt very homesick. Not for any particular place, as I no longer identified with a physical location, but for the boat herself. After more than two years of wandering under sail, my home was wherever MOON-SHINER lay waiting. But the work in Indonesia took longer than expected, and it was to be almost three months before I saw her again.

BATWING

Our marina on the IJssel was old, but its location was ideal—far enough upriver from Rotterdam to give it a distinctly rural feeling but still close enough for Lot to have easy access to her job in the city. It also boasted a powerful crane capable of supporting MOONSHINER's heavy weight, and we were able to haul her out of the water at a reasonable cost to make our own repairs and paint the hull. Most of our neighbors lived aboard converted river barges and shallow draft powerboats, and for the first year we were the only full-keel sailboat in the facility. But at the end of our second summer we lost our exclusive status when Lloyd and Judy arrived aboard BATWING.

"How're you doing?" asked Lloyd as I helped him tie up. "Fine," I replied, admiring his unusual boat. The Stars and Stripes were flying on a traditional hull but she was junk-rigged, Chinese style. "Where are you from?" "A whole bunch of places," he said. "But our home port's Seattle." "In that case we're almost neighbors. We're heading back to Vancouver," I replied. He was tall, over six feet, and had the sturdy physique and bearing of a man still in his prime. We learned later that he was 72, but it wasn't in his nature to let age or any other obstacle slow him down.

Lloyd didn't learn to sail until he was approaching retirement in his early sixties. At 69, the waters around Seattle no longer provided enough excitement and he decided to circumnavigate the globe singlehanded. Judy let him go, thinking perhaps that his enthusiasm for the venture would soon fall victim to the reality of life in a small boat on a big ocean. But by the time he reached Tonga she wisely changed her mind—before he had time to find a girl in every port—and jumped on a plane to join him. They'd completed the crossing of the Pacific together, and then followed the same track as MOONSHINER through Asia, the Middle East, and the Mediterranean.

As neighbors in the marina we soon became good friends, and a few weeks after their arrival Judy announced "We're flying back to the States for the winter, but we'll be back in the spring to take BATWING across the Atlantic. Why don't you leave with us in MOONSHINER?" "We'd love to but we haven't saved enough money yet. It'll take us at least another year before we're ready," Lot replied. While they were away we kept an eye on BATWING, and when they returned in the spring we helped Lloyd rig the boat. We stood on the dock and waved goodbye on the day they left. When they were out of sight I jumped into the car and drove several miles downstream to watch them pass. I didn't wave again—they didn't know I was watching—but how I longed to follow them. Soon they would feel the warm tropical trade wind at their backs, be visited by dolphins and entertained by flying fish as they sailed westward into the sunset, with the promise of the Caribbean beyond. If sailing is a drug I was badly addicted, and I wasn't looking for a cure—only another fix.

We received regular reports on their progress by mail, and celebrated for them when we heard that they had reached Acapulco, and Lloyd closed the circle on his circumnavigation. They left the boat in Mexico for a couple of years to return to the States, and then Lloyd returned to BATWING and sailed her from Mexico to Hawaii and then on to Alaska, where Judy joined him again for the final leg of the journey down the coast to Seattle. By then MOONSHINER had arrived in Vancouver, and they visited us on their way south. Lloyd was getting close to 80, but if Judy hadn't dissuaded him I have no doubt he would have set off once again across the Pacific.

One night, the winter after Lloyd and Judy left Holland, we lay in bed listening to the howl of the wind as it swept unchecked out of the North Atlantic and across the frozen February landscape of the Maas River Delta. The boat shuddered in protest at the storm, but what intimidated us most wasn't the wind but a different sound. A sound that grew louder as the night wore on—the sound of ice groaning against the hull. "It can't be doing the boat any good," observed Lot with mild understatement. "I think it's trying to grind its way into the boat." We were locked into the ice as securely as Shackleton's

ENDURANCE. It was over a foot thick, and a few days earlier we had given up the losing battle of trying to keep the boat free by chipping at it with an axe. Our neighbors told us it was the coldest winter for a decade. It had certainly been too much for the colony of cockroaches, which had defied all our efforts to get rid of them since they first hitched a ride in Borneo. We hadn't seen one for months, and I didn't think they were hibernating.

In the middle of the river the channel was kept open by the continuous flow of barge traffic. But nearer the banks the ice had broken into large floes, which exerted considerable pressure against our hull whenever a vessel passed by. To make matters worse the river was tidal, and near low water we sat on the bottom as the level continued to fall several more inches. The ice would then close tightly around the hull, and try to lift MOONSHINER out of the water on the next flood. As we lay in bed, listening, it sounded as if the hull might crack open like an eggshell at any moment. "I can't stand it any longer," Lot finally announced. "Tomorrow, I'm going to arrange for the boat to be cut free." "And how are you going to do that?" I inquired. "I'll see if the hotel gardener will come over with his chainsaw," she said. "He's not got much to do at this time of year, and he could probably use some extra money."

The gardener arrived the next day. He soon realized he had accepted a nightmare assignment and within minutes he was soaked, head to toe, in ice-cold water. But he persisted, and a couple of hours later we were free. We hauled the boat later that spring and carefully checked for any sign of damage to the hull. There was none.

As a dog raised in the tropics, Fluke had mixed feeling about the Dutch winter. She had never seen snow before, but she soon discovered that it could be fun. Ice, on the other hand, was a different matter. She was never able to comprehend that it was now possible to walk on water; as far as she was concerned the stuff surrounding the boat was supposed to be liquid, and if we were crazy enough to risk stepping onto it she certainly wasn't going to follow. But the cold winter temperatures didn't seem to bother her. On returning to the boat one particularly frigid afternoon she ran down the dock to meet us as soon as she heard our footsteps. We assumed that she had spent the day in MOONSHINER's warm cabin, where we had left her, but as we walked along the frozen dock towards the boat we were shocked to see the frost-free outline of her body silhouetted on the planks, legs and paws outstretched in her favorite position. She must have been lying there for hours, patiently waiting for us to come home as the frost slowly built up around her. But if she was cold she didn't show it as she led us back to the boat with her tail wagging happily.

Winter eventually gave way to spring, and with the melting of the snow the call of the sea grew stronger. After almost three years in Holland we had finally saved enough money to get MOONSHINER in shape for another ocean crossing, and we began planning our journey home.

23. Getting Ready

Five months before our expected departure date, Lot passed on some unwelcome news, "The marina's been sold and we've got until the end of the month to find somewhere else to live." "Who'd want to buy it?" I wondered aloud. "The place is about to sink." "It's been bought by developers, and they're going to tear it down and build houses along the riverbank," she said. Rumors that the owners were hoping to sell had been circulating around the marina for months, but we'd hoped to be able to hang on until we were ready to head to sea the following spring. It was now late November, so with winter fast approaching we had to find MOONSHINER a temporary home. We were lucky. After searching for several days we discovered a yacht club in the old port of Hellevoetsluis that agreed to give us a berth.

Our departure for Hellevoetsluis was quite an adventure— it was the first time that MOONSHINER had left the marina in two and a half years. With her deep keel and low horsepower she wasn't very suitable for navigating the inland waterways of Holland, and we preferred to explore the country by road anyway. To reach the North Sea, the closest place where we could have done any real sailing, required a 30-mile journey through one of the busiest industrial waterways in the world. So we preferred to keep MOONSHINER secured to the dock while we planned our next voyage to less crowded and *warmer* destinations.

The journey to Hellevoetsuis took us through the industrial

heart of Rotterdam. MOONSHINER sped rapidly downstream as watery sunlight fought to break through the mist. The trees and well-tended gardens along the riverbank soon gave way to cement-grey warehouses, office buildings, and commercial docks as we approached the city. We bucked and rolled in the wake of huge barges that were hurrying upstream with cargoes of raw material to feed the industrial appetite of factories along the Rhine. Between Rotterdam and the open sea lies the largest container terminal in the world: Europort, where a forest of dockside cranes towers—each like a watchful preying mantis—over thousands of ocean-going ships. But we soon left the city and the main river channel behind, and passed into a network of canals which cut through farmland dotted with hamlets and small villages, and in the middle of the afternoon we arrived at our new home.

We worked hard that winter getting MOONSHINER ready for her Atlantic crossing. All her gear and every piece of equipment were carefully inspected, or so I thought, and on a sunny spring morning we were ready to take her for a shakedown sail on a nearby lake. To get to the lake we had to pass through a lock, and just as we were about to join the queue of boats waiting their turn our steering suddenly failed. We drifted slowly towards the bank until a nearby boat saw our predicament, took us in tow, and delivered us ignominiously back to the berth we had left only a few minutes earlier. After a quick inspection I discovered the "key" holding the steering wheel onto its shaft had fallen out. I replaced the screw holding it in place—this time applying lots of goop to keep it in place.

To Sea at Last

The big day finally arrived. After bidding farewell to family and friends we passed through the final lock leading into the North Sea and headed south, along the coast of Belgium towards France and the English Channel. We arrived at Calais on a falling tide, and were obliged to anchor for several hours until the next high water lifted us high enough to pass through the lock leading into the town's small-boat harbor. Unfortunately, after years of cruising in areas with very little tidal movement we were unprepared for the huge rise and fall of the tide in the Channel. MOONSHINER sank lower and lower, and the depth sounder made it clear that if it didn't stop soon we might be lying on our side in the mud. I grabbed the tide table and set about looking up how low it was going to go—something I should have done earlier. I calculated that we would just touch bottom, but as the seabed was soft we decided to stay where we were. We spent a tense hour as her bottom settled several inches into the ooze before the flood tide came to our rescue.

A few hours after leaving Holland I had noticed a leak in the thru-hull fitting that discharges MOONSHINER's cooling water and engine exhaust. So the day after we arrived in Calais I spent a couple of hours struggling, unsuccessfully, to unscrew it. Nothing worked. Try as I might it wouldn't budge. I braced myself against the hull and pulled with all my might using a large wrench, I hit it with hammers, soaked it with penetrating oil, poured boiling water over it and finally, in frustration, turned a propane torch on it. All to no avail—it might as well have been welded in place. Defeated, I gave up. "I'll go and find the harbor office. There must be someone nearby who can help," Lot said. She returned in less than an hour with a plumber and his assistant. I pointed out the offending fitting and the plumber crawled into the engine room without waiting for me to explain that all means of extracting it, short of using explosives, were doomed to failure. I heard one loud *clunk* and in less than a minute he was back in the cabin, holding it in his hands and smiling. "Ask him how he did it," I said to Lot, impressed. "Ah Monsieur, à chacun son métier (to each his trade)," he said wistfully.

The weather in the Channel was unsettled for mid-summer, and we decided it was wise to wait in port for a suitable window before we set out across the notoriously rough Bay of Biscay bound for Spain. But our patience paid off, and we were rewarded with a fine four-day crossing to La Coruña, in light to moderate winds. We cruised the rocky coastline of Galicia for several weeks, and then sailed slowly south towards Portugal, arriving in Lisbon in the middle of September.

Into the Atlantic

We left Lisbon bound for Porto Santo early one morning at the end of September. The weather was sunny, and a brisk northerly wind promised a speedy passage. "With a bit of luck we should make it in about four days," I said to Lot. The wind held steady throughout the day, and MOONSHINER was at her best in the 20-knot breeze, averaging a steady six knots. But in the middle of the night the wind veered into the northeast and began to strengthen, and at dawn it was blowing 30 knots. "Let's heave-to for a while and cook breakfast, " I suggested. "Maybe it'll ease up. This wasn't in the forecast." But it didn't, the wind grew stronger, and by the time we'd finished eating it was blowing almost a full gale. We remained hove-to for a couple of hours, but even when the wind stabilized at just over 30 knots I felt reluctant to get underway. We had experienced much worse conditions in the past, but that was over three years ago, and in the meantime we'd lost our sea legs and I felt apprehensive. Finally, I realized that if we waited for conditions to improve we could remain sitting there for days. "The wind's not going down but it isn't getting any stronger either, and it's blowing in the right direction," I said. It was time to shake off our fears. "Let's get moving," Lot replied.

The wind continued to blow at near gale force from directly astern for the remainder of our second day at sea, but although the ride was rolly and uncomfortable we were making great progress in the right direction. We gradually became reaccustomed to the big seas, and apprehension gave way to exhilaration as we rushed towards the southwest, surfing occasionally on top of the larger waves with a scrap of foresail and a double reef in the main. At around three in the afternoon Lot shouted "Look, a plane," and as I turned a large Portuguese military aircraft roared past, skimming low over the water. It was so close the pilots in the cockpit were clearly visible. We waved. "I guess they're just checking that we're OK," I said. "Either that, or they're bored." "They probably just think we're crazy to be out here," said Lot. Later that same evening the wind began to go down, and by midnight it was back to a much more comfortable 20 knots. We shook out the reefs and for the next two days enjoyed a beautiful sail under clear skies, making a steady six knots all the way. At dawn, four days after our departure, we dropped anchor in the small stone harbor of Porto de Abrigo, four kilometers from the Vila Baleira, the tiny capital of Porto Santo.

In the early 1400s, Portuguese explorers began pushing further and further down the west coast of Africa. It was during this period that the Atlantic islands of Porto Santo, Madeira, and the Canaries, which had been known to the mariners of antiquity, were rediscovered. But like many landfalls during this age of exploration, their discovery owed more to serendipity than to navigational skill. In 1418 a Portuguese *barca*, sailing in search of Guinea, was caught in a storm, blown off course, and accidentally discovered the island of Porto Santo. This led to a follow-up colonizing expedition in 1420. But the expedition's leader, in a well intentioned but ill-conceived initiative, took along a pregnant rabbit and released her and her offspring onto the island—presumably in the expectation of nourishing rabbit stews and an ample future supply of furs. Fortunately for the rabbits, but unfortunately for the settlers, the island had no predators. There were no diseases to which rabbits could easily succumb, but there were abundant quantities of suitable food. The inevitable result was that they multiplied as only rabbits can, and devoured everything in sight, including the crops of the settlers—who were forced to flee for their survival to the neighboring island of Madeira.

In 1480, a young Christopher Columbus came to Porto Santo to buy sugar. He fell in love with the governor's daughter, and spent two years living on the island before moving to Madeira where he studied navigation—a skill which he was to put to good use twelve years later. The house where he lived while in Porto Santo is still standing in Vila Baleira.

Although extremely arid, the island is beautiful. We spent hours walking with a very happy Fluke along miles of deserted golden beaches, bordered by the deep blue of the Atlantic on one side and the rugged low-lying volcanic hills of the interior on the other. Inland, the vegetation was dry scrubgrass and miniature cactus, but if the land was still home to the descendants of the prolific rabbits they were keeping out of sight.

Madeira

When Porto Santo was first discovered, the captain left some men behind for the winter while he returned with the rest of the crew to the mainland. On clear days Madeira was easily visible and the crew realized their island was part of a larger archipelago. In contrast to its smaller neighbor, the island of Madeira had a much higher rainfall and when the first settlers arrived it was covered with trees. In an attempt to clear the land the trees were set alight, but unfortunately the fires grew out of control and it is reported that the fires burned for a total of seven years, adding wood ash to the natural volcanic ash found on the island. When grapevines from Crete were planted to replace the forest they flourished in the ash-rich soil producing the unique strong wine for which the island was to become famous. The settlers also planted sugar cane, and by 1460 the island had become the biggest single producer of sugar in the western world.

Madeira's high mountain terrain and beautiful coastline make it one of the world's most beautiful destinations. Flowers and fruit trees seem to flourish everywhere, and the brilliant red bougainvillea, jacaranda, orchids, bird of paradise plants, and orange and lemon trees add to the natural beauty of the island. Over the centuries settlers built terraced fields in the steep mountainous terrain which are supplied by water through irrigation channels known as *levadas*. Paths along these channels provide unique walking access to the interior of the island, and they have become renowned amongst hikers for their unique beauty.

24. Kidnapped

"I have to go into town for supplies," said Lot. "Do you want to come along?" We were hurrying to leave for the Canary Islands to take advantage of a good weather forecast. A brisk northeast wind was driving a choppy sea into the congested harbor and MOONSHINER was performing her usual crazy rolls. "I don't like leaving the boat alone in this. You go ahead and take Fluke and I'll finish off some jobs here." "OK, I shouldn't be more than an hour." When one hour became two, and then three, I wasn't too concerned—I assumed she had run into friends in the town and probably gone for coffee. Nevertheless, it was with some relief that I finally saw the dinghy come bouncing out of the inner harbor and head towards the boat. Fluke, as usual, sat happily balanced on the bow enjoying the flying spray. But as they got close I could see that Lot was upset and shaking her head. "We never came closer to losing Fluke," she said as she climbed aboard. "It's a miracle we got her back." "Sit down and tell me what happened," I replied.

"When I got to the supermarket, I tied Fluke up as usual to the bike stand, just outside the main door. There were lots of people going in and out and I didn't expect to be very long. But inside the store was really crowded, and because it was taking longer than I expected I kept walking to the door to check that she was OK. The first couple of times I looked she was fine, but the next time I checked she wasn't there. She'd disappeared. My first thought was that her leash must have come undone and she'd just wandered off. But when I began shouting her name a man stopped to tell me he'd seen a woman untie a dog a couple of minutes earlier and walk away with her. He didn't know which direction they'd gone. At that point I began to freak out." "I'm not surprised. What did you do then?"

"I figured that in a couple of minutes they couldn't have gone very far, so I ran up and down all the nearby streets shouting 'Fluke, Fluke' at the top of my voice and asked everyone I met if they'd seen a large dog. I was frantic, and everyone must have thought I was crazy." "But you don't speak any Portuguese. How could they understand you?" "I know enough to ask if they'd seen a large dog—a perro grande," said Lot. "And anyone could see I was desperate. Anyway, Fluke had completely disappeared. Finally I met a couple of teenage girls who were giggling together on a street corner, and when I asked them if they'd seen a dog they looked uncomfortable and then nodded. I asked 'Where? . . . which direction?' but they just shrugged and pointed vaguely down a nearby street. I took off again, running as fast as I could in the direction they'd pointed. But there was still no sign of Fluke. I was really desperate now and thought we'd never see her again. I went back to the street corner and the girls were still there. I tried asking them one last time, because I felt sure they knew something they weren't telling. 'Please . . . the dog . . . which way?' They looked at each other without speaking and then one of them pointed in a completely different direction from the street where I'd been searching. She pointed to a four-story apartment building just across the road.

"I ran into the building but there was nobody to be seen, and no sign of Fluke. I realized my only chance of getting her back, if she was inside, was to create a real ruckus. So I ran up the four flights of stairs to the top floor and started screaming 'Fluke . . . Fluke,' as loud as I could, while ringing all the doorbells. If they thought there was a mad woman loose in the building they were right. Then I heard someone talking on the floor below. I leaned over the stairwell balcony and I could see two women talking in front of an open door . . . and standing between them was Fluke." "Good grief, you were lucky." I said.

I looked over at Fluke, who was already asleep in the cockpit and unimpressed by her adventure. "What did you do then?"

"I ran down the stairs to find out what had happened. I couldn't understand most of what they said, but I didn't really care—I was so relieved at finding Fluke. I think the woman from the apartment was trying to say she found the dog wandering the streets, and decided to take her home. The second woman lived in the same building, and walked with me back to the lobby. On the way, she shook her head and made a grabbing gesture to indicate that she thought Fluke had been stolen. She must have noticed her neighbor arriving in the building with an animal she hadn't seen before, and when I went crazy I guess she put two and two together and figured out that the dog had been stolen. I think she knocked on the woman's door to tell her the foreigner wasn't going away, and she'd better give the dog back."

Losing Fluke would have been like losing a family member. We'd shared so many adventures together that life aboard MOONSHINER without her was unimaginable. We would have spent years wondering what had happened to her, and whether or not she was still alive. Fluke had grown into a beautiful looking animal, and although she was six years old people often mistook her for a large puppy. Perhaps that's why the woman took her, but we'll never know. We just resolved to keep an even closer eye on her in future.

The Canaries

We dropped anchor at Tenerife, the largest island in the Canaries archipelago, in mid-afternoon after an easy two-day sail from Funchal. The islands have a rich and colorful history spanning almost two millennia, but for over a thousand years, memory of their existence faded into European folklore. It wasn't until the late thirteenth century that a Genoese captain confirmed their existence when he landed at the island that would later bear his name, Lanzarote. In 1341, King Alfonso IV of Portugal sent three ships in search of the rumored "islands in the sea." When they reached the Canaries they discovered they were already populated by a race of tall, blonde, blue-eyed natives who called themselves Guanches. Their origin remains a mystery, but given the reputation that European explorers would soon establish for butchering indigenous populations it was a black day for the locals. Only four of them were captured by the first Portuguese ships, but over the next century they were systematically massacred, or sold into slavery, by a succession of invaders.

The landscape of Tenerife is dominated by the snow-capped peak of Mount Teide, which at just over 12,000 feet is the third highest volcano in the world. Up close, the fantastic rock formations and strange topography just below the summit make you feel as if you've arrived on an alien planet rather than a tropical island—an observation that wasn't lost on the Hollywood director who filmed the movie *Planet of the Apes* under Teide's shadow. It's the contrast between the alien landscape near the summit of the volcano and the tropical beaches of the shoreline that gives the island its unique appeal. But it's an appeal that has been undermined by shoddy-looking tourist developments that have been cobbled together all over the island without regard for preserving its natural beauty. But a euro, or a pound note, will buy you an English beer—and fish and chips which you can consume on the beach while listening to a cockney DJ on the radio, if that's what you want.

The Order of the Paintbrush

When leaving Holland, Lot had packed a supply of paintbrushes, with the idea that she might pass the time on longer passages by learning to paint. She never did, but one day she rediscovered them while cleaning up the boat, and they gave her an idea. "I think we should have an award that we can present to some of the interesting characters we meet," she announced.

"What kind of an award?" I asked. "Well, something that we can give to people who we think are particularly unusual in some way. People who seem to make the most out of their own lives and in the process render life more colorful for those around them." "Sounds great," I said. "There're no shortage of candidates around here. What could we call it?" "How about the order of the paintbrush," she replied. "We could string them on colored cord, so they could be worn as pendants, and make up cards saying *You have been awarded the Order of the Paintbrush—for adding color to our lives.*" And so the international *Order of the Paintbrush* was born.

The first recipient was Maurizio. He was a Sicilian and a Buddhist—in itself a fairly rare combination—about 30 years old. He had been living on his trimaran in Las Galetas for a couple of years. He'd built her in Portugal, and then sailed her singlehanded to the Canaries. When he started the project he didn't let the fact that he knew nothing about boats or sailing deter him; he just learned as he went along. He seemed to have a ready supply of beautiful vacationing girlfriends, whom he regularly entertained, and his income came from Asian artifacts—such as rugs and inexpensive jewelry—that he sold on the sidewalk in the town. "Where do you get them from?" I asked him one day. He laughed. "I buy them in Santa Cruz at a wholesaler and just mark up the price by 20%. They're really popular. I don't get rich but I make a good living. And it's a great way to meet girls," he added with a grin.

La Gomera

A few miles to the west of Tenerife, the small rugged volcanic islands of La Gomera, La Palma, and El Hiero stand like mountainous sentinels. In the Middle Ages they marked the western edge of the known world, and in 1492 Columbus chose La Gomera as the departure point for his voyage into the unknown. It was while provisioning his ships on this island that Columbus, a widower of 41, fell in love with the beautiful

Beatriz de Bobadilla, who had been a childhood friend of Queen Isabella of Spain.

Despite their friendship, Beatriz's good looks and allure had caused her problems at Isabella's court. Rumor has it that the queen didn't take kindly to her husband's growing interest in her erstwhile friend. So she arranged for Beatriz to be married off and placed safely out of the king's reach as the wife of the Governor of La Gomera. Her husband was later murdered in an uprising by the island's Guanches, and Beatriz was forced to flee with her children. But after the rebellion was brutally put down, she assumed the role of Governor herself. Unfortunately, her good looks belied a cruel nature, and her subsequent rule was not a happy one for the islanders. But Columbus was obviously smitten by the charms of the 32-year old widow, and he visited her on two subsequent trans-Atlantic voyages. It was only after she married someone else, during one of his long periods of absence, that he finally crossed her off his Atlantic travel itinerary.

We decided it would be fun to follow in Columbus's footsteps and make La Gomera MOONSHINER's last stepping stone into the Atlantic. Roughly circular in shape and only 15 miles in diameter, the island's mountains soar to almost 5,000 feet. Their summits are frequently shrouded in mist and cloud, and their moisture supports a lush laurel rain forest that covers the deep and impenetrable ravines which radiate outwards from the island's center. It is the greenest and least populated island in the Canaries. But it attracts fewer visitors than its neighbors; the wetter climate and absence of beaches has limited tourism, and most visitors are day-trippers from nearby Tenerife.

We tied up in the marina at the island's small capital, San Sebastian, and spent a couple of days making final preparations and topping up our supplies for the Atlantic crossing. Many of our neighbors were friends from Tenerife or Madeira who were about to embark on the same voyage, and conversations around the dock focused on weather reports, and what kind of sea conditions we could expect. It doesn't matter how far you've sailed, crossing the Atlantic in a small boat is still a big deal, and anybody being honest would have admitted to some apprehension. The day before our departure we rented a car and drove along the steep winding and deserted roads that cut into the island's interior. Spectacular mountain views were interspersed with brief stops for coffee in small lazy mountain villages. I loved the island and wished we could stay longer—partly because of the natural unspoiled beauty of the place, and partly because I suspect I secretly wanted to delay our appointment with the Atlantic.

On our last evening we visited the site of the church that Columbus and his crew attended the night before their departure. Though old, the current building is not the original church—which was destroyed 100 years after Columbus's death. But it was a good enough facsimile for our visit to feel symbolic. Unlike Columbus we didn't believe divine intervention could influence our voyage one way or the other. But it was thrilling to feel that we really were following in the footsteps of the great explorer—his adventure had been successful and ours would be too. We left San Sebastian at five o'clock on the afternoon of December 8, and motored out of the marina into a flat calm sea and our first Atlantic sunset.

25. Ocean Crossings

Our choice of early December as a departure date—two months later than Columbus—was no accident. The hurricane season in the Caribbean lasts from June until November. August to the end of October is the worst period, with September the peak month. Columbus didn't know it, but by leaving at the beginning of September he was playing Russian roulette with the weather gods—who chose to be kind to him.

The light wind that accompanied our departure soon picked up to a comfortable 15 knots out of the northeast, and we made fine progress. Or at least we made fine progress for the first four days. "We've got a leak," I announced to Lot as I crawled out from under a bunk after a routine inspection of the hull. "How far are we from land?" was her sensible reply. "About 400 miles, give or take," I replied. There was a moment's silence. "Don't worry," I added, trying to be encouraging. "It's not big. It's just a pinprick hole and there's so little water coming in you could soak it up with blotting paper." But she didn't look very reassured.

The question was—what should we do now? Should we hold our course, or steer for the Cape Verde Islands for repairs? I knew MOONSHINER's steel hull was basically in excellent shape. The leak was in a small area of rust that I'd discovered a couple of years earlier and treated by scraping and repainting the metal. I thought the problem was solved, but the corrosion had obviously eaten further into the steel than I'd imagined. The amount of water coming in was tiny, but it was in a highly

stressed part of the hull, close to the skeg—the small vertical
keel that supports the rudder. The hole was minute, but how
thick was the remaining metal in its vicinity? Would the leak get
bigger before we reached Barbados? And what if we ran into
bad weather—was the hull weakened to the point where we
might be risking the loss of the skeg and the rudder? Probably
not, but with over 2,000 miles of ocean still to cross I wasn't
sure I wanted to take the chance. We talked it over, weighing
our options. "OK, let's head for the Cape Verde," I said at last.
"They're almost on our course anyway. Better safe than sorry."
Four days later we dropped anchor in the harbor at Mindalo on
the island of São Vicente.

São Vicente

The island was dry and barren. Really barren. No vegetation
grew on the desolate red-brown hills that watched over the blue
water of the harbor, with its cluster of small dirty freighters and
ancient fishing boats. Children played on the beach in front of
the town, and behind the beach a row of tired-looking palms
and small shrubs looked incongruous in the otherwise lifeless
landscape. Behind the town center, small grey shanties leaned
against the lower slopes of brown rock. Mindalo, even in the
bright mid-afternoon sunshine, looked as if it was half asleep,
and in its lethargy it lacked the will to shake off the coating of
sand and dust the relentless Harmattan wind had deposited on
its journey from the African desert to the Atlantic. It was a hot
and thirsty wind—a wind that sucked the moisture out of the
ground and baked the earth. Mindalo was poor.

At the customs office we asked where we could get the boat
repaired. They pointed in the direction of a commercial marina
on the outskirts of the town. After a long hot walk we arrived,
tired and thirsty, to find the place deserted. We were about to
leave when a shout made us turn, and we saw a figure emerging from an aging fishing boat. It was a young African, aged
about 25, wearing a ragged blue T-shirt, dirty khaki shorts,

and tattered sandals held together with pieces of string. "Hello, can I help you?" he asked. I stopped. Surprised, not by the question but by the trace of an English accent. We explained what we were looking for. He shook his head. "There are no welders here. You could try CABNAVE," he said, pointing to a shipyard across the bay on the far side of town. "They weld big boats. They might do it." "I need a rest before I go anywhere," I said to Lot as I sat down on a pile of wood. He came over and sat next to me. "Do you work here?" I asked. There was a long pause. He stared at the horizon for a long time before he replied: "I don't work here. I don't work anywhere. There is no work."

"How do you survive?" I asked. "A friend lets me sleep in his boat," he said, nodding in the direction of the rotting craft from which he'd just emerged. "But what about food," I asked again. There was another pause. "I get enough food," he said, but he didn't elaborate. Finally, he took his eyes off the horizon and turned to face me. "Do you know any sailboats going to Gambia? I have to get off the island but I have no money. I can sail. I would be good crew. Do you know anybody?" Each year a few cruising sailboats stop at the Cape Verde as part of a detour to visit the West African country of Gambia before setting out across the Atlantic, but we hadn't met any in the anchorage. "I don't. We've only just arrived. But why Gambia? You sound as if you could be English?" He smiled, shaking his head. "I was born in Scotland, in Glasgow. My mother lived there for a while. She was from Gambia and my father, whoever he was, worked on a freighter. My mother went back to Gambia and took me with her." "Do you have a Cape Verde or English passport?" I asked. "Neither. That's why there's no work for me here. There isn't much work for anyone, and they won't hire an outsider."

He told us his story. As soon as he was old enough to get a job, he had signed up as crew on a freighter working the ports between the west coast of Africa and Europe. He enjoyed the work and the roaming lifestyle. He had a little money in his pocket, and he thought he had escaped the poverty of his childhood home. One day, when his freighter was lying at anchor in the harbor in São Vicente, the captain told him they were reducing the size of the crew and he would have to lay him off—he was out of a job. "But surely he couldn't do that," I said. "There must be some rule that prevents shipping companies from marooning their employees." He shrugged. "Nobody cares. Maybe where you come from it's different, but here nobody cares. He told me lots of ships visit Mindalo and I'd find another berth. But it isn't true, nobody wants to hire crew here." "Did you have any money saved?" He laughed, as if the question was stupid—which it probably was. He turned away and stared again at the horizon. "Just before I left the boat he gave me an envelope. Inside was a hundred-dollar bill. Damn him. Why did he give me a lousy hundred dollars? So I could stay here and suffer? Why did he do that?" I had no answer.

We visited him several times during our stay; brought food, and assured him we were spreading the word amongst the cruising boats that he was looking for a berth. But the sad truth was that nobody was eager to take on an unknown crew member. I believe that at least some of his story was true, and finding a passage on a boat heading for West Africa seemed the only way out of his sad predicament. When we left the island a couple of weeks later he was still there.

The CABNAVE shipyard was equipped to haul out mid-sized freighters and ocean going fishing boats onto its slipways, but anything less than a thousand tons created a problem; they had no method of lifting a small boat out of the water. "The only way I can get you ashore would be to custom-build a cradle. And that would cost you about $4,000, not counting the welding." We were talking to the young yard manager, but it looked as if it was going to be a short conversation. Our limited budget whispered that for that amount of money we would soon be taking our chances again with the ocean, leak or no leak. We were about to leave when he offered another solution. "We could weld on a doubling plate underwater, that way we wouldn't need to haul you out." I didn't even know that underwater welding was possible—it sounded like an oxy-moron. I resisted asking him why the water didn't put out the flame, or how the welder avoided electrocuting himself. Instead, I asked if it would be strong enough and how much it would cost. "There's no problem with the strength," he replied, and then, after a short pause to think: "We could do it for two hundred US dollars, it would only take a couple of hours." "You have a deal," I said, relieved.

The next day we hauled in the anchor, motored over to the shipyard, and tied up alongside the company's dock. It wasn't long before a van carrying four men, including two welders, arrived on the scene and began unloading equipment. Everyone was laughing and joking and seemed to be in a party mood; I guess working on a sailboat was a novelty that broke the daily routine. Unfortunately, their good humor was destined to be short lived. One of the welders, who spoke a little English, quickly organized his equipment, donned his diving gear, and disappeared under the hull to take a look. We followed his trail of bubbles with interest. Finally, he reappeared looking worried. "Not easy. The boat moves too much," he reported. He was not a gentleman given to overstatement. The wind seemed to be blowing harder than ever that morning, and there was a lively chop on top of a moderate swell in the exposed harbor—not a factor if you're working on a 5,000-ton freighter, but MOONSHINER was rolling and bucking as if she was competing in a rodeo!

He grabbed his welding gear and disappeared back into the water, while a couple of his colleagues went aboard MOON-SHINER to make sure that nothing caught fire. After half an hour he surfaced to take a short break. "How's it going?" I asked. "Slow," he replied as he dropped back into the water. He didn't look happy. After another half hour of struggle he was exhausted and his colleague took over. After that they took it in turns, each working in 30-minute shifts. Finally, after about three hours, they announced that they had finished. But they were barely out of the water when a shout from inside the boat announced that water was still coming in. I went to take a look.

What had been scarcely a trickle before they began work, had grown significantly. Scraping and cleaning the hull to prepare it for welding must have widened the original hole, and the plate they had just welded over it obviously wasn't waterproof. They struggled for several more hours to find the flaw in their welding and make the repair watertight. But although they managed to reduce the flow, a small trickle obstinately persisted. By this time it was getting late in the day and the yard manager had arrived on the scene. "We'll finish it off tomorrow and we'll weld a backing plate inside the hull to make sure you don't have any more problems," he announced.

Next morning, with the wind still blowing and MOONSHINER still bucking, the welders arrived with their cheerful smiles temporarily restored and disappeared below deck to start work. The result was predictable. The tossing boat was soon redolent with the suffocating stench of welding fumes, burning paint, and sweat. Our heroes, working head down in the bilge, didn't stand a chance. In less then ten minutes they were forced to retreat, gasping, onto the deck; their smiles gone, their faces now whiter than their teeth. After a few minutes rest and a few deep breaths of sea air, they headed below to try again—bravely confronting the inevitable. Five minutes later they were back on deck. We expected them to quit, but with an effort above and beyond the call of duty they disappeared for a third time, only to emerge less than two minutes later, totally defeated. Reinforcements were urgently summoned.

Like their predecessors the new men arrived in a cheerful mood. In ignorance of the fate that awaited them, they took great pleasure in taunting their unfortunate comrades who were still sitting on the wharf recovering from their ordeal. Gallantly, the new crew disappeared into the inferno and we waited, fascinated, to see how long they would last. Our answer came in less than ten minutes as they staggered out of the boat and onto the dock. In the meantime, the men who had arrived earlier were now sufficiently recovered to begin wandering off, mumbling phrases which we interpreted to mean things like: "other urgent work," and "back later," or a prophetic "finish tomorrow." It was obvious that ten minutes of effective work each hour was all that anyone could accomplish, and as a result the work wasn't finished until noon the following day.

The job that was only going to take "a couple of hours" had lasted almost three days and we expected the worst as we entered the office to pay our bill. "Two hundred dollars is what we quoted you, and two hundred dollars is the charge," said the yard manager as he looked at us rather ruefully. He earned our profound gratitude at that moment, and his shipyard added two members to its international fan club. We had no further problem with leaks, and when we hauled the boat a year later in Mexico to clean and paint the bottom, the welding still looked excellent.

South America, because of the cultural connection, is a favorite destination for cruising sailboats from Portugal or Spain. And amongst the friends we made in the anchorage at São Vicente was the young crew of a Spanish boat that was heading across the Atlantic to Brazil. On board were a newlywed couple, and the wife's younger brother. They spoke excellent English and we enjoyed many hours in their company. "How was your crossing from Spain?" I asked one evening. Everyone except the husband, who was the captain, started to laugh. "What's so funny?" I asked. "I get seasick," he groaned. "There's more to it than that," said his young brother-in-law, still laughing. "We only had one period of bad weather, and our illustrious commander immediately got sick and then disappeared. We found him lying in his bunk." "It's true," he grinned. "I told them I thought we were going to die, and if that was the case at least I was going to die in bed, and to hell with it."

We spent the last few days in Mindalo shopping to replenish our food supply. The market was well stocked with a good selection of fresh fruit and vegetables, and we even found a small store selling frozen chickens—presumably for the benefit of the few tourists on the island. We planned to spend Christmas in the middle of the Atlantic, but I was determined that this wouldn't prevent us from enjoying a Christmas dinner, complete with all the trimmings. In the Canaries I'd stocked up with stuffing mix, canned cranberries, fruitcake, plum pudding, and gravy mix. With a frozen chicken under my arm, I now had all the ingredients for my mid-Atlantic feast. Lot thought I was mad.

The parties we had enjoyed with our Spanish friends had seriously depleted our liquor supply, and I didn't want to emulate the US Navy by completing the voyage as a *dry* ship. We inquired where we could buy more alcohol, and were directed to a small private house in a narrow back street. We knocked on the door and a couple of minutes later an old lady was escorting us down into a cobweb-draped cellar in which were stored row after row of dusty, unlabelled, five-gallon jars containing a clear water-like liquid. "I think we've found the source of the local moonshine," I said to Lot. "Ask her what brand she's selling— Hatfield or McCoy." "When US customs see the name of our boat, they'll figure we're exporting the stuff. Are you sure you want to risk drinking it?" The old lady probably understood English better than I realized, because she immediately poured us both a sample. It smelled a bit like paint thinners but to my surprise it didn't taste too bad. "It'll do," I said. "We can always mix it with fruit juice, and if all else fails it's probably great for killing cockroaches—it must be a thousand percent proof." So for less money than we normally paid for a bottle of wine, we walked out of the cellar with a full gallon of Mindalo's finest elixir. The next day our friends left for Brazil, and two days later we followed them into the Atlantic and pointed MOONSHINER's bow towards Barbados—2,000 miles to the west.

26. West with the Sun

We departed Mindalo on Lot's birthday, two days before Christmas. As soon as we left the protection of the harbor we were greeted by the full force of the northeast trade wind as it accelerated around the island and chased the short steep coastal waves into the Atlantic. The wind whistled in the rigging and the sea hissed as MOONSHINER came alive, spread her sails, and dipped her bow into the spray. With the wind on the quarter she rose effortlessly to each wave as it raced up from astern, and then chased after them—as eager as they to reach the horizon and discover what lay beyond. I was happy and excited, but also apprehensive as I thought about the miles that lay ahead. The trade wind was so strong that to turn around in an emergency and beat back against the current would have been impossible. We were on a one-way roller coaster, and like it or not the next stop was Barbados. Slowly, as the brown dust-dry hills of the island receded into the distance, I grew accustomed to the rhythm of the waves and began to relax. We were re-entering the beautiful and addictive world of the blue-water sailor.

Out of sight of land we inhabit a small and private world. A world bounded by the nearby horizon—less than three miles away—the dome of sky overhead and the ever changing sea below. By day, if the weather is good, we float at the center of a sparkling blue cocoon and at night we keep watch under a Milky Way that glows with stardust. We measure the passage of time in sunrises and sunsets, and by the changing phases of the moon. Our world bears no resemblance to the ocean viewed from land, when it's easy to be intimidated by its immensity and the apparent absence of life. From the deck of a small boat the ocean shrinks, develops a personality, and comes alive. It transforms into a self-contained world in which visiting birds, dolphins, and other creatures make it easy to feel at home and unexpectedly secure. They seem to be masters of their fate, following their own paths. Perhaps we share a common spirit. "Follow us, follow us," laugh the dolphins as they tire of playing in the bow wave and speed off into the distance in answer to some unknown call. "Follow me," urges the sun, as it hangs for a moment over MOONSHINER's bow before sinking, in a blaze of color, into the western horizon.

Two days after leaving São Vicente it was time to prepare the Christmas feast. For the previous 48 hours the trade wind had remained fresh. It blew night and day at between 20 and 25 knots, more than enough to drive MOONSHINER at her hull speed. The only disadvantage with downwind sailing is that it's impossible to stop a boat rolling from side to side, and during the passage from São Vicente to Barbados we estimated that we rolled almost half a million times. Conditions like this make preparing a gourmet dinner something of a challenge. But persistence—"sheer cussedness," according to Lot—paid off, and I was in the last stages of serving it onto plates when we fell off a particularly large wave. Chicken, Brussel sprouts, stuffing, baked potatoes, cranberry sauce, and gravy flew across the cabin and landed against the far wall in front of a startled Fluke. Determined not to let this little mishap ruin a perfectly good meal I quickly scraped it up and put in back on the plates, before Fluke had a chance to decide that it was some sort of airborne Christmas treat. "How is it?" I asked Lot. "Fine," she replied loyally, as she picked a dog hair out of her mouth.

Columbus

In the two days since leaving São Vicente, MOONSHINER had traveled almost 300 miles into the Atlantic. But two days after leaving La Gomera on his first voyage, Columbus, plagued by light winds, was still in sight of the Canary Islands. His goal was to reach Cathay (China), Cipangu (Japan), and the spice markets of the Indies by sailing west rather than around the southern tip of Africa. The geographers of his day knew that the earth was round, but they drastically underestimated its size. He was advised that China lay only 3,000 miles from the Canary Islands, but in reality it's 9,000 miles further than that. It was his great good fortune to bump into America, or his departure from La Gomera would have been the last anybody saw of him. Nobody in Europe, with the possible exception of a few aging Vikings, knew that America existed. And after his triumphant return to Spain, Columbus was still convinced that he had landed in Cipangu.

His log of the voyage has not survived, but we have a summary of it written 40 years later by Bartolomé de las Casas, a Dominican friar whose father had sailed with Columbus on his second expedition. It shows that for the first ten days things went well, and the crew were optimistic. On their tenth day at sea Las Casas reports: *"The Admiral says that from this time they experienced very pleasant weather, and that the mornings were most delightful . . . they began to meet with large patches of weeds, very green, and which appeared to have been washed away from land . . . they all judged themselves to be near some island, though not a continent, according to the Admiral, who says 'the continent we shall find further ahead'."*

MOONSHINER also continued to enjoy pleasant weather, and the wind remained strong out of the northeast. We rocked and rolled towards our destination at an exhilarating speed, occasionally surfing for an instant on the crests of the bigger waves while the rotor of our water generator—towed behind the boat on a 100-foot line—repeatedly jumped out of the water and skipped over the surface of the sea. But the Atlantic is a wide ocean, and despite our speed the line showing our daily progress on the chart moved very slowly.

We have found that a useful way to break the routine of a long passage is to divide it up into bite-sized pieces by heaving-to for a couple of hours every two or three days, in the late afternoon, to enjoy a *happy hour* and prepare a leisurely meal. We tell each other we "have arrived" at some temporary en route destination. The technique of heaving-to is normally used when the wind and sea conditions become too much to handle. When properly hove-to a boat will normally take care of itself, even in the worst weather, and enable its exhausted crew to re-tire below and wait out the storm in relative comfort. But even in good weather it's useful as a way to relax and enjoy a change of pace, and we consider the extra few hours it adds to our pas-sage as time well spent.

We never touched the helm throughout our entire Atlantic crossing. From Mindalo to Barbados, MOONSHINER steered her-self on autopilot. And navigation was also easy, thanks to GPS: which gives a more accurate indication of where I am at sea than I've ever had on land—particularly after a good party. But I made a point of keeping my sextant skills intact by calculat-ing a noon fix and comparing it with the GPS position—just in case a lightning strike got a little too close. But for Columbus, navigation wasn't such a simple affair.

Columbus navigated by "dead reckoning": regularly calcu-lating his speed by dropping a floating object overboard at the bow and timing how long it took to reach the stern. He could combine this information with his knowledge of the boat's course to plot an updated position on his chart. But after they had been at sea for 11 days they were shocked to discover the compass seemed to have gone crazy. "*The pilots . . . found that the needle varied to the north-west a whole point of the com-pass; the seamen were terrified. The Admiral discovered the cause, and ordered them to take the amplitude again the next morning, when they found that the needles were true; the cause was the star moved from its place."*

The "error" was caused by magnetic variation. A compass needle points towards magnetic north—a point located in northern Canada—not true north. As they sailed towards the west, the compass pointed further and further to the east. This would have been apparent to anyone on board who compared the compass needle with the location of the Polaris, the North Star, which remains stationary in the sky directly above true north. In a deft feat of salesmanship, Columbus convinced his crew that it wasn't the compass that was *wrong*, but that Polaris was now rotating around the sky like other stars. He benefited from the fact that people tend to believe what they desperately need to believe.

On September 23, their seventeenth day at sea, they *". . . saw a turtle dove, a pelican, a river bird and other white fowl; weeds in abundance with crabs among them."* But the crew were not reassured: *"The sea being smooth and tranquil, the sailors murmured, saying that they had got into smooth water, where it would never blow to carry them back to Spain."* Two days later *". . . Martin Alonzo called out with great joy from his vessel that he saw land . . . The Admiral . . . fell on his knees and returned thanks to God . . . Those on board the Nina ascended the rigging, and all declared that they saw land."* But they were to be cruelly disappointed. The next day it became apparent that what they had mistaken for land was only cloud.

In fact they were nowhere near land. By steering a westerly course for Cipango, Columbus was approaching the Sargasso Sea, an area of warm water in the western Atlantic. The weeds that they took as a signs of land, were nothing more than the floating algae for which the Sargasso Sea is famous.

On October 10, after 34 days at sea—32 of them out of sight of land—Columbus was forced to appeal to the crew to avoid a mutiny: *"Here the men lost all patience, and complained of the length of the voyage, but the Admiral encouraged them . . . representing the profits they were about to acquire, and adding that it was to no purpose to complain, having come so far, they had nothing to do but continue on to the Indies."* The following day the crew of the Pinta saw a log in the water, and the crew of the Nina saw a stalk loaded with rose berries. Finally, *". . . two hours after midnight . . . the Pinta . . . discovered land and made the signals which had been ordered. The land was first seen by a sailor called Rodrigo de Triana, although the Admiral at ten o'clock that evening standing on the quarter-deck saw a light, but so small a body he could not confirm it to be land."* The date was October 12, 1492. Columbus had discovered the New World and the rest, as they say, is history.

The line showing MOONSHINER's position on the Atlantic chart may have moved slowly, but at least it moved towards a destination whose existence wasn't in doubt. Early in the morning on January 7, after 16 days at sea, we sighted land, and that evening we dropped anchor in Carlisle Bay, Bridgetown. No history books will record the event, nobody was there to greet us, and our arrival had little impact on anybody—but it was one of the greatest moments in our lives. We too had sailed across the Atlantic Ocean.

27. The Caribbean

The Caribbean is justifiably famous for the beauty of its islands, its unmatched climate (except for the hurricane season anyway), idyllic beaches and clear blue water. But although we enjoyed our stay in upbeat Barbados—it was our favorite island in the Caribbean—as we journeyed south through the Grenadines we began to feel strangely out of place. The islands are a playground for thousands of American and European visitors, but the dollars and euros that they bring have little impact on the lives of most local people who remain impoverished. All too often the slums begin within a stone's throw of the back door of the expensive resort or the five-star hotel. The enormous income gap between tourist and islander has led to a bitter resentment towards visitors that borders on open hostility. In the Caribbean, as in many other countries we've visited, the warmest welcome and happiest memories are reserved for the traveler who seeks out the small town or village far away from the tourist centers.

We enjoyed our best Caribbean cruising in the sun-drenched, wind-blown, and isolated islands off the coast of Venezuela: Los Testigos, La Blanquilla, Las Aves, and the Los Roques Archipelago. Lying between 60 and 100 miles from the mainland, most are inaccessible except by boat and development has passed them by. Many are uninhabited except by the fishermen who make them a temporary home during the fishing season. Even in the larger islands, where a few fishing families have permanently settled, we often went for days without seeing a fellow human being. The anchorages were usually deserted, and then we had only ourselves, the cry of the pelicans, the murmur of the wind, and the sound of the low breaking surf for company. In the evening the pelicans would rest and the wind would sometimes become calm—and then there was only silence, and the sunset, and time stood still.

We walked for hours with Fluke on deserted beaches of white sand that glared blindingly bright under the tropical sun. And we watched, entertained, as pelicans plummeted vertically into the crystal clear turquoise water to catch fish. Their airborne skills were superb, but on the ground they became gangling incompetents. Landing appeared to cause them particular problems. Their approach speed seemed too fast, and when they hit the ground their legs failed to keep up with their bodies and they collapsed onto the sand in a thrashing tangle of legs and wings. They would slowly pick themselves up, give a big shake, and then waddle away looking very annoyed. We hiked into the interior of the islands. They were arid and covered with a mix of dry grass, small shrubs, and cacti. In the middle of one, which we thought was deserted, a strange noise made us suddenly turn. A donkey was eyeing us suspiciously from behind a bush. After a few minutes he decided we weren't a threat, and his mate appeared with a young foal. Where had they come from? How did they find water? Did anybody own them? We had no real idea, but assumed that they must be wild.

We had been anchored in Yaque Bay on the island of La Blanquilla for a couple of days when a small but pretty looking sloop of about 35 feet arrived and dropped anchor. She wasn't new, in fact she looked as if she had a good many miles under her keel, but she had simple classic lines that still caught the eye. An hour later we heard the sound of their dinghy being launched and a few minutes later it bumped up against MOON-SHINER's hull. Lot said, "Hello, come aboard." In typical yachtie fashion we were soon swapping stories with her crew. The skipper was a middle-aged Belgian woman, and her partner was a young athletic looking islander she had met while cruising in

Martinique. "I like your boat," I said. "Ah yes, it was designed by the Argentinean German Frers. It was the first in its class and he used to own it himself." "Did you buy it in the Caribbean?" I asked. "No," she replied laughing. "I got it from my husband in the divorce. I know it's the husband who normally gets to keep the boat, but I thought it would be more fun the other way round. So I gave him the house." We all laughed. "Have you been sailing for long?" I asked. "Not really. My husband used to do most of the sailing. He was the expert, but we're learning as we go along." She smiled at her young partner.

"Where are you heading next?" she asked. I told her we were leaving the next day for Los Roques. "Oh, so are we," she exclaimed. "Can I ask you a big favor? Can we follow you to make sure we don't get lost?" "Yes," I said, puzzled. "But why would you get lost? Why do you need to follow us?" She looked embarrassed. "Well, to tell the truth, we don't know how to navigate." "Don't you have a GPS?" I asked. "They tell you exactly where you are. There's nothing to it." "No. We keep meaning to buy one but we never seem to get around to it." I looked at Lot, who was shaking her head in amazement. "But how did you get here from Martinique? It's hundreds of miles away." "We sail from one island to the next, and usually we can see from one to the other," she replied. "If they're further apart we just wait until someone is going in that direction and ask if we can follow." I resisted the temptation to say the fortune doesn't always favor the foolish, and instead said "OK, we'll call you on the VHF radio tomorrow a half hour before we leave, so we can both be ready at the same time." "Oh, I'm very sorry but we don't have a radio," she replied, apologetically. For some reason I wasn't surprised.

Our destination in the archipelago of Los Roques, Crasqui Island, was 130 miles to the west, and in the strong trades that meant a journey of just under 24 hours. As soon as we saw them raising their anchor the next morning we did the same. It was blowing 25 knots, and in the ten minutes it took to get everything securely stowed for the journey we were well over a mile from the anchorage. "I think they have a problem," said

Lot, who had been keeping an eye on them with the binoculars. "Here, have a look," she said, passing them to me. Back in the anchorage it was obvious that they still hadn't moved, and their foresail seemed to be flogging back and forth out of control. We held our course for another ten minutes, expecting at any moment to see them sort out the problem and follow us. But the sail continued to flog. "We'd better go back and see what's wrong. We can't just leave them," said Lot.

By now almost half an hour had passed since our departure and we were three miles from the anchorage. Even motorsailing it took us well over an hour to beat back into the bay against the wind and current. We arrived to find that they had re-anchored and finally managed to roll in the foresail. They were sitting on deck looking tired, and more than a bit shaken. "What was the problem?" I shouted as we came alongside. "We couldn't furl the foresail. The wind was too strong." I was puzzled. They had a roller-furling system—the sail was rolled in and let out by pulling on a furling line attached to a drum beneath the sail, and it should have been easy to control—it works on the same principle that makes a cotton bobbin rotate when you pull on the thread. "Is your furling gear broken?" I asked. "Yes, it's never worked." I thought their capacity to surprise me was over. But I was wrong. When I looked more closely at their reefing gear I saw that there was no reefing line attached to the drum at all. "How do you try to reef?" I asked. "By hand," said her young friend. "It works OK if the wind isn't very strong, but it gets impossible if it's blowing hard." I pointed out, "Unfortunately that's exactly when you need to reef." He had been trying to roll up 400 square feet of madly flapping sail by twisting the furling gear by hand. "Why didn't you just drop the whole sail?" I asked. "Because we can't get it down. It's stuck."

We now had a predicament on our hands because we felt responsible for them. They were obviously a disaster waiting to happen. At least I was able to show them how to jury-rig the sail so that it would only unfurl a small amount—better too little sail than too much, I figured. "Would you like to try again tomorrow?" I asked. "Maybe there'll be less wind." With a look of profound relief they agreed to postpone their departure until the following day. "Their only hope is to get to Bonaire, get the boat fixed, and buy some navigation gear," I said to Lot later that evening. "The only direction they can sail is downwind." "How far is it?" she asked. "About two hundred and fifty miles. If they want to follow our itinerary I guess we should offer to lead them." Lot looked doubtful—neither of us was looking forward to the prospect of rescuing them from further disasters on a daily basis. The next day we offered to accompany them to Bonaire but they declined. "Just help us get to Los Roques, that's all we need," they insisted.

The wind was slightly less strong when we left the next day, but not by much. My main concern was that we might lose them during the night: with their foresail heavily reefed, and with no easy way to adjust it without the risk of the whole thing coming lose, their speed would be slow. But the big reef turned out to be a wise move, as by midnight the wind was gusting to 30 knots. To keep their navigation lights in sight MOONSHINER was reduced to a triple reefed main and a deep reef in the genoa. But we managed not to lose them, and at dawn they were still clearly visible about a mile astern. We reached the islands at about eleven o'clock in the morning and hove-to, waiting for them to catch up. "Thank you. Thank You," they shouted as they sailed past—heading for a different part of the archipelago, "See you in Bonaire."

But we never saw them again. Months later, we heard that they had successfully reached Las Aves Islands where the woman had contracted a serious case of paralyzing ciguatera fish poisoning. Her partner had managed to get the boat to nearby Bonaire where she could receive treatment. After she recovered they set off again, heading west, but their boat had been wrecked on a reef and was a total loss. Both of them had luckily escaped with their lives.

We spent a week exploring the beautiful islands of Los Roques Archipelago—where the water was the most brilliant turquoise we had seen since leaving the Red Sea—before pressing on to Las Aves and the ABC Islands: Aruba, Bonaire, and Curaçao. We were beginning to feel a sense of urgency and the need to make progress. It was already late in March, and we had to make sure that we were out of the hurricane zone before the next cyclone season began. This meant arriving at the southern tip of Mexico's Baja Peninsula before the end of June. And another concern was the rumor that fees for small boats using the Panama Canal would soon be increased, and we wanted to make sure we completed our transit before it happened.

The western corner of the Caribbean, close to Panama, is notorious for its strong winds. Many world cruisers have experienced the strongest winds of their entire circumnavigation in this region. So we waited patiently in Aruba, the most westerly of the ABCs, for a good weather forecast before embarking on the 600-mile passage to Colón at the entrance to the Panama Canal. Our patience paid off, and by local standards we enjoyed a relatively easy passage. But when we were about 15 miles from our destination we passed close to a small freighter heading in the opposite direction—against the wind and heavy seas. "We've got to be crazy," said Lot as we watched its labored progress. As the boat met each wave its bow lifted high out of the water before crashing back in a deluge of white water and flying spray, its propeller regularly coming half out of the sea. MOONSHINER, heading downwind, rode the large waves comfortably and this made it difficult to appreciate how big they really were. Three hours later we anchored near the yacht club in Colón.

Panama

We were warned not to venture out of the grounds of the marina after dark. The town is notoriously dangerous, and robbery, particularly of tourists, has become something of an art form. We met two yachties whose handbags had been snatched by passing motorcyclists in broad daylight. Colón is a town in a time warp—the American West of the 1880s or Chicago in the 1930s. The door of the local supermarket was guarded on the inside by two men with pump-action shotguns; I guess it doesn't matter how many customers are cut down by the spraying lead, as long as the perpetrators of any crime don't make it out into the street in one piece.

In contrast to the squalor of Colón, the Panama Canal is marvelous. It's hard to avoid unkind comparisons between the world's two great canals. The Suez is cut through the featureless Egyptian desert, and the pilots who came onboard MOONSHINER were corrupt. The Panama is cut through the lush tropical hills of the isthmus, and its pilots were unfailingly professional, polite, and a pleasure to be around. The Panama Canal Authority was still under the control of the US at the time of our transit, but the pilots and all the other officials that we met were local Panamanians. Each cruising boat is required to have four line-handlers, as well as a skipper and pilot on board. So the usual procedure is to help as a line-handler on someone else's boat before making the transit yourself. This gives you the opportunity to get a feel for how everything works and learn what to expect. The biggest problem for small boats is that the system wasn't designed to handle them. The rate at which water flows into the massive locks is so fast that a small boat can easily get out of control in the turbulence unless it is firmly secured by lines to the lock walls, or it is tied up next to another secure vessel. But on both our line-handling trip and our own transit we went through without mishap—as part of a raft of three or four other sailboats.

In the canal MOONSHINER traveled in the company of a magnificent 38-foot sloop that was being delivered from a shipyard in New England to her new home in Acapulco. During our two-day passage I took time to admire the impeccable cabinetry in her cabin; all her wooden table surfaces were covered in beautiful marquetry designs, and the seats and other vulnerable fittings were carefully wrapped in layers of plastic to protect her from the elements and wear and tear by the crew. She was a floating work of art. "What did she cost?" I couldn't resist asking. "One point three million" the skipper replied. "Good grief," I said, "that's almost fifteen times what we paid for MOONSHINER, including the cost of re-fitting her, and she's the same size." The beautiful woodwork in the American boat suddenly seemed a very expensive luxury.

After two enjoyable days in the canal we passed under the Bridge of the Americas, and anchored in front of the Balboa yacht club. We had arrived in the Pacific.

In the great oceans of the Northern Hemisphere the prevailing winds follow a clockwise and roughly circular path, like a disc rotating on a giant turntable. In the high latitudes of the North Pacific, the most common winds are the westerlies that blow from Asia towards North America. As they approach the coast they take on a more southerly slant, and blow out of the northwest towards Mexico and Central America. Further south, on the far side of a region of variable wind, lies the zone of the Northeast Trades where the winds blow back towards the Pacific. A boat leaving the west coast of Canada or the United States, bound for Mexico or the South Pacific, can expect to make a fast downwind passage. In fact the conditions are usually so ideal that this southbound route is known as the "Coconut Milk Run" because of its reputation as a downhill tropical sleigh-ride. But the northbound journey, from Central America to the Pacific Northwest, is a very different story.

The direct route from Panama to British Columbia follows the coast, and promises a 5,000-mile difficult slog against the prevailing wind and current. The alternative is to make a wide detour into the Pacific, perhaps stopping in Hawaii, before finally heading north and then east, towards North America. But to reach Hawaii meant an offshore passage of at least five weeks, and if we wanted to go ashore we'd have to put Fluke into quarantine kennels. So after studying the pilot charts we decided on a compromise: we would head up the coast as far as

San Diego, and then make a smaller and less demanding off-shore detour.

The beginning of our journey was deceptively easy as we motorsailed in light winds and a calm sea along the coast of Panama and Costa Rica. The shoreline was beautiful and un-spoiled. We traveled in short hops, spending no more than a day at sea before seeking a quiet anchorage to relax, enjoy the solitude, and admire the lush tropical rain forest. But as we traveled further north the headwinds and adverse current grew progressively stronger, and it took MOONSHINER 20 days to cover the 1,100 miles from Panama to Puerto Madero, just inside the Mexican border.

Mexico

"I'm not looking forward to cruising in Mexico," Lot an-nounced soon after our arrival in Puerto Madero. "Are you worried about the headwinds?" "No. I think it's going to be a bit like the Mediterranean. An expensive tourist trap." I had my own misgivings, but we made an effort to avoid marinas—we couldn't afford them anyway—and tried to find small anchor-ages well away from the tourist hot spots. We discovered lots of them, and soon decided that our earlier reservations about the country had been unwarranted.

We reached Cabo San Lucas at the southern tip of the Baja Peninsula in early June. We were anxious to get further north before the onset of the hurricane season, so after only one night in the anchorage we continued up the coast towards Ensenada, a port just south of the US border. It was an exhausting 800-mile uphill slog against the current and against headwinds that regularly blew at 20 knots and occasionally much higher. The journey took just over three weeks—sailing close to the shore during the day and usually anchoring at night. Our sense of ur-gency was increased when the ham weathernet warned that an early tropical disturbance was slowly moving up the coast in our direction. We knew that the only southerly wind we were likely to encounter at that time of year would be the leading edge of a storm, so we kept moving as quickly as possible. The sailing wasn't easy, but we enjoyed the isolated and beautiful peninsula—with its wild desert coastline and large sea lion colonies. We vowed that one day we would return, but on our next trip we'd be heading south—with the wind.

The USA

With 3,500 miles of Pacific in her wake since leaving Panama, MOONSHINER finally arrived at the police dock in San Diego to be inspected and undergo the entry formalities for the United States. Since we had left Hong Kong, where MOONSHINER was still registered, the colony had reverted back to Chinese rule and I wondered how the US authorities would react to our legal ensign—the flag of the People's Republic of China. "It might be good idea not to fly it heading up the coast," was the only comment it prompted from the officials. "It might be misunderstood." We stayed at the police dock for ten days, which was the maximum they would allow. Its location—near marine stores and shopping facilities—was ideal, and we discovered that their moorage charges were the lowest in town. And as an added bonus we didn't have to worry about security.

After the boat had been inspected we walked to the customs office near the center of town. When we arrived the waiting room was empty, and the agent was standing behind a customer-service window absorbed in making entries in a journal. "We're here to check in," I said. "Give me a minute," she replied without looking up. There was a long pause, and then with her nose still buried in the journal she asked: "Where are you from?" "We just arrived from Mexico. But we're really from Holland, or at least most recently we're from Holland." "What nationality?" she asked. "I have two passports, Canadian and British, and my wife is Dutch." "Where is your boat registered?" she asked, still without looking up. "China," I replied. "Well, actually it's Hong Kong. Hong Kong is now a part of China but when the boat was registered Hong Kong was British. So she was originally a British boat registered in Hong Kong, but now she's Chinese." "Where was it built?" she asked. "Australia," I replied. At this point she finally put down her pen and looked up. "My God, who *are* you people?" she exclaimed. But she wasn't a woman who was easily rattled, and a few minutes later the paperwork was satisfactorily completed.

Into the Pacific

Our plan on leaving San Diego was to head out into the Pacific in a wide arc, gradually altering our course towards the north as soon as the wind direction permitted, and then approach the coast again when we reached the westerly winds of the higher latitudes. The pilot charts for the North Pacific—which show the average wind strength and direction for each month of the year—indicated that such a route was feasible provided we got far enough offshore and out of range of the relentless northwesterlies.

We left the harbor in a flat calm that we later decided had been sent to tempt us into further folly. The breeze soon picked up and before long we were making good progress. On our second day at sea the wind increased in strength and by the third day it was blowing so strongly out of the northwest that we were being pushed well to the south of our planned course. The going was rough, wet, and miserable, and against the steep seas our progress became painfully slow. The marine weather forecasts weren't encouraging either; they made it clear we would have to travel at least 400 miles before we could expect more favorable winds. And to add spice to the adventure we heard that another tropical disturbance had just been upgraded to a tropical depression and was heading up the coast in our direction. "They hardly ever get this far north but we don't want to get pushed any further to the south," I told Lot.

By late the following afternoon the wind was gusting over 30 knots and had backed further into the west. Conditions were awful and MOONSHINER made little headway as she slammed into the high steep waves. We hove-to and drifted slowly to the southwest while we debated what to do. Should we wait and hope that the forecast was wrong, or cut our losses and head back to the coast. I looked at the chart. "Right now we're about 250 miles offshore, and at the same latitude as Ensenada." I told Lot. "How much further is it to Vancouver?" she asked. "About 24,000 miles—if we keep heading in this direction we'll have to circumnavigate," I replied cheerfully. "The wind is pushing us towards the South Pacific, not British Columbia." We decided to turn around. Like most tough decisions, once you've made them they immediately seem like the right thing to do and you wonder why it took you so long to make up your mind.

We wanted to motorsail in order to claw our way as far to the north as possible, but when I turned the ignition key the engine turned over but refused to start. I waited a few seconds and cranked it again with the same result—no engine. I released the compression levers to turn her over by hand and heard the familiar and depressing sound of water sloshing around in the cylinders. I crawled reluctantly into the crazily rolling torture chamber that we call an "engine room" and began the long, hard, and nauseating task of getting the water out of the engine and back into the ocean where it belonged. "What happened?" shouted Lot from the entrance door. "Water leaked in from the exhaust pipe. The seacock wasn't completely closed." I started the job at six in the evening. The engine finally started at two o'clock in the morning, by which time I was almost beyond caring.

We turned the boat around, and two days later we dropped the anchor at San Luis Obispo. We were only 200 miles north of San Diego, but we'd added over 500 miles to the log. It had been quite an excursion.

29. The Journey Home

Ten days later we sailed under the Golden Gate Bridge and tied up at a marina in San Francisco Bay. We were tired of doing battle with the constant headwinds and decided to take a break for a couple of weeks, soak the salt-spray out of our bodies, and explore one of the world's great cities. The marina was full of boats that had sailed down the coast from Washington or Oregon and were waiting for the hurricane season to end before continuing south to Mexico. All of them had made fast passages, and the old hands reported that the northwesterlies were blowing much stronger than normal. A sturdy 45-foot sloop arrived from Seattle, bound for the South Pacific. They had experienced near gale force conditions the whole way and were still nursing their wounds—which included a broken boom and torn sails. "Good grief, and they were going *with* the wind," said Lot. We had obviously chosen a bad season to be heading north.

We left San Francisco in early September, and a few days later we tied up alongside the fishing fleet at the Noyo yacht basin in Fort Bragg. Our arrival had been exciting; the coastline only emerged from a thick blanket of fog when we were a mile from the shore, and the heavy swell broke angrily on the jagged rocks that flanked the narrow entrance channel as we neared the mouth of the Noyo River. Without our GPS and radar we would have had no option but to remain at sea until conditions improved. Even with our modern electronic aids the approach was intimidating, and it was a relief to finally reach the security of the marina. But we soon discovered that our newfound security was in jeopardy from a small colony of sea lions that had decided to make the yacht basin their home. They made it clear that they didn't welcome visitors, and they scowled at us angrily as we hurried quickly past on our way to the marina office. "We can't get rid of them," apologized the manager. "They're an endangered species protected by law. Don't get too close. They can be aggressive, and they move pretty fast when they want to. They've already chased a couple of people down the dock."

Mendocino

Fort Bragg lies 70 miles south of the biggest natural obstacle faced by a yacht beating up the west coast of the United States—Cape Mendocino. Located halfway between Canada and Mexico, the notorious landmark thrusts menacingly into the Pacific and marks the fulcrum where the coastline of the continent changes direction. To the south the land turns towards the southeast, and holds that course for 1,300 miles, all the way to the southern tip of the Baja Peninsula. But on the other side of Cape Mendocino the coastline of Oregon and Washington points north towards Canada. A few miles east the coastal mountains soar to over seven thousand feet, and faced with this barrier the northwesterlies are diverted from their path and pick up speed as they accelerate around the obstacle.

We were sick and tired of beating to weather, but the end of our journey was almost in sight. We had put 4,500 miles on the log since leaving the Panama Canal—20,000 miles since leaving Hong Kong—and once past the Cape only 500 miles would separate us from Vancouver: three days sailing under normal conditions. But conditions were far from normal. We sat in Fort Bragg listening to the whine of the wind in the rigging and waiting for a break in the weather. We visited the nearby coastguard station to ask their advice—if anybody knew this part of the coast, they did. "It's been a bad season, but even at this time of year you should get a break if you're patient." So we spent a couple more days relaxing, avoiding the sea lions, and enjoying the old town while we waited for the wind to ease up. Finally the weather forecasts began to sound encouraging, and we got ready to conquer the last big obstacle.

We left just before noon on a warm sunny day with only a 5-knot breeze rippling the sea. By nine o'clock that night we were only 25 miles from the Cape, and the wind was still less than ten knots. "I think we're going to make it," I said. "Vancouver here we come." I should have known better than to tempt fate. Two hours later it was still blowing at only ten knots but then in less than half an hour the wind built rapidly to 30 knots, gusting to 35. It was like running into a wall; the wind came out of nowhere—one minute we were under full sail and using the engine to help boost our speed, and the next we were struggling to put three reefs in the main. The waves increased in height almost as quickly as the wind picked up speed. And they were nasty steep waves, and in combination with the strong southerly current they stopped MOONSHINER in her tracks.

I said to Lot, "We'd better heave-to. We're just pounding the boat and not getting any further north." So we spent the rest of the night in sight of the Cape, hoping the wind would ease just long enough for us to claw our way past. But by dawn there was no sign of any improvement, so we reluctantly turned around and ran back down the coast. Three hours and 20 miles later we dropped anchor in appropriately named Shelter Bay, and collapsed gratefully into our bunks.

Two days later the wind started to ease again, and as we prepared to get underway for another assault on the Cape it became dead calm, and then a light zephyr sprang up out of the south. We couldn't believe our luck—only 30 miles to the Cape and a favorable wind. If the conditions held, we would be in Oregon in just a few hours. We tiptoed out of the anchorage—anxious not to wake the fickle weather gods—and by ten o'clock that night we were back in our old position, 25 miles from the Cape, and the breeze was still blowing out of the southwest. I went below to plot our position on the chart, and after a couple of minutes I heard the sound of the wind increasing. I assumed that we were just getting a stronger push in the right direction, but when I went back on deck less than five minutes later the wind had veered to the northwest. It was already blowing 20 knots and increasing in speed by the minute.

This time the wind wasn't content to limit itself to a mere 35 knots, it had greater ambitions. We hove-to with a triple reefed main and the merest scrap of foresail, and watched the wind speed indicator unwind like an F-16's altimeter on take-off: 30 . . . 35 . . . 40 . . . 45. The wind was no longer moaning—it was screaming, and raging white horses were foaming down on us out of the pitch-black night. "Let's get out of here. This is crazy," I said to Lot. We eased the jib onto the other tack and bore away, surfing the waves at eight knots. The wind speed indicator showed 45 knots gusting to 50, but we were running downwind so its true speed in the gusts must have been closer to 60.

Suddenly there was a loud bang as if the rigging had given way and the mast was about to be torn from the deck. I looked up. All that was left of our triple reefed main were a few scraps of white Dacron plastered around the spreaders and the mast. The rest had quite literally been blown into shreds. The loss of the sail made no difference to our speed and we continued to surf downwind towards the protection of Shelter Cove. "It's got to improve soon, as soon as we get clear of the Cape it should go down just as quickly as it came up," I said to Lot. But it didn't. The wind remained above 40 knots out of the northwest until we were less than five miles from the anchorage when the altimeter began to wind down. Four miles from the bay it dropped to 30 knots . . . three miles out it was down to 20 . . . two miles out it was only blowing at ten and the seas started to calm. Twenty minutes later we rounded the headland protecting the cove in a dead calm, and dropped the anchor into water that was barely rippled and with no sign of a swell. We have often encountered accelerating winds near islands and headlands, but this experience had been unique.

It was getting late in the season and we were faced with a major decision. We sat in the coffee shop at Shelter Cove and carefully weighed our options. We could either wait where we were and tackle Mendocino again if the weather gave us a break. Or we could call it a day and look into the cost of shipping the boat by road to Seattle. The only other alternative was to spend the winter in San Francisco and head up the coast the following spring.

The idea of giving up on our assault on Mendocino Cape was hard to take. We had sailed two-thirds of the way around the world—much more if you counted the actual miles we had put on the log—and the idea of giving up 500 miles from home was hard to stomach. But unless we got past Mendocino quickly we would end up tackling the remainder of the journey in October or November, and the early fall had been bad enough. Captain Cook—a man not lacking in knowledge of the ocean and its ways—said that some of the worst weather he'd ever encountered was off this stretch of coast in the winter. Along the flat coastline between Oregon and Canada the only anchorages that give protection in bad weather are located in rivers. But the irony is that in bad weather they are inaccessible because of the deadly surf that breaks over the sand bars at their entrance—in conditions when the bar is "breaking" the coastguard won't even let you try. Of course they're perfectly accessible in good weather, but in good weather you don't need to get in.

After much discussion, Lot said, "Well, I think we've given it our best shot. We're in danger of trashing the boat and it's the only asset we have left. I think we should look into shipping her by road." It was a hard decision, but I was inclined to agree. We had a spare mainsail—it had come with the boat—but our finances were precarious and we didn't have the resources to pay for any more major repairs. We looked up *marine transport* in the yellow pages of the phone book and called a San Francisco number. We were quoted a price of around $3,000 to Seattle. "Let's try a company that's based in Seattle," Lot suggested. "Maybe they have a truck that's returning empty and they'll give us a deal." Her hunch paid off. After twenty minutes on the phone she was quoted a price of $1,500. "That's less than we'd spend cooling our heels in California for the winter, even if we lived like hermits," I said. "Let's do it."

"How much does your boat weigh?" asked the hoist operator as he lifted MOONSHINER out of the water to load her onto the truck. "Between twenty and twenty-five thousand pounds, or at least that's what the builder told us," I said. "I don't think so. I think you're closer to thirty," he replied. We hoisted her onto the truck and the driver looked suspiciously at the tires— which suddenly seemed a lot flatter—but he didn't say anything. It was a Thursday morning, and after helping him strap her down we arranged to meet early the next week in Seattle. As soon as he left we got a ride into town, rented a car, and drove north through the California wine country. Rain started to pour down almost as soon as we left the city limits, and it continued in a deluge that was the main news story on the radio for the next two days.

The weather improved just before we reached Seattle. We phoned Lloyd and Judy—who'd temporarily left BATWING in Mexico—to let them know we'd arrived and they came down to the marina for a reunion. The truck arrived on schedule, and we were relieved to see MOONSHINER safe and sound. But stacked on the trailer beneath the boat were two blown out tires. "She sure was heavy," is all he said when he saw me looking at them. We lowered MOONSHINER back into the water and I lifted the hatches in the cabin sole—just to make sure no water was coming into the boat before they disconnected the lifting harness. "My God," I yelled through the hatch, my mouth suddenly dry. "We're sinking. Lift me up. There's two feet of water in the bilge!" The hoist lifted us out, but to my surprise the water level in the hull remained the same. If that much water had entered the boat in a couple of minutes it should logically have drained out just as fast. But it didn't.

Then I understood. I had closed the seacocks that empty the cockpit and deck drains before the boat left San Francisco.

In three days of torrential rain, all the water that had landed on the boat had run through these drains, backed up into the sink, and then overflowed into the hull. No wonder he'd blown a couple of tires—there must have been two tons of water in the boat.

Home Again

MOONSHINER seemed none the worse for her overland adventure, and with Lloyd's help we stepped her masts and prepared her for the last leg of her long journey. It was hard to believe that we were almost home and our adventure would soon be at an end.

We spent a week slowly cruising the final miles between Seattle and Vancouver. We were reluctant to travel more quickly—aware that a magical time in our lives was coming to an end and reluctant to speed up the process. The protected water of Puget Sound and the Strait of Georgia were calm and welcoming as we ghosted past the islands where, long ago, I had first experienced the freedom that is sailing. We watched silently as the coastal mountains broke clear of the haze. And as we rounded Point Grey, the city of Vancouver came into view— looking as beautiful as I remembered. Off the starboard beam, less than half a mile away, lay the beach that Lot and I had visited so many years ago when I left the small hospital room that I had shared with Karl: the beach where our dream began.

Epilogue

A light drizzle dripped from the trees bordering the marina as we tied up the boat—she looked lost and sad on the rain-slicked rickety dock. There was nobody to meet us. It was eleven years since we had left Vancouver and I was a stranger again in the city that would always be my home. Our finances were precarious, we were no longer young, neither of us had jobs, and our closest friends were scattered to the four corners of the earth. MOONSHINER was our only possession. But we had made our choice and followed our dream—and the choice had been good. I remembered a day 30 years earlier when I had arrived at the train station with $100 in my pocket. I looked at Lot and smiled. It was time to set out again and re-discover a new continent.

> *We shall not cease from exploration*
> *And the end of all our exploring*
> *Will be to arrive where we started*
> *And know the place for the first time.*
> T.S. Eliot